THE NECESSITY FOR RUINS

GF
91
.U6
J32

Jackson, John Brinckerhoff

The necessity for ruins,
and other topics.

DATE DUE			
~~DEC 08 1993~~			

THE SIDNEY B. COULTER LI
ONONDAGA COMMUNITY COLLE
RTE 173, ONONDAGA HILL
SYRACUSE, NEW YORK 1321

D0061130

JOHN BRINCKERHOFF JACKSON

THE UNIVERSITY OF MASSACHUSETTS PRESS   AMHERST

THE
NECESSITY
FOR
RUINS

AND OTHER TOPICS

Two of these articles originally appeared in
Landscape, and are reprinted by permission. "The
Domestication of the Garage" was published in
Volume 20, Number 2 (1976), pp. 10–17.
"Landscape as Theater" was published in Vol-
ume 23, Number 1 (1979), pp. 3–7.

LC 79–23212
ISBN 0-87023-291-6
Printed in the United States of America
Library of Congress Cataloging in Publication Data
appear on the last page of this book.

Contents

Learning About Landscapes

For more than twenty years I spent many months
going from college to college to speak to groups of students
about American countrysides and American towns and cities.
I had travelled widely in the South and Midwest and Southwest, and I enjoyed telling a more or less captive public what
I had seen and how I thought towns and countrysides had
become the way they were. Very poor slides served to illustrate
my remarks. If I remember rightly it was in the mid-fifties, at
the University of California at Berkeley, that I began this itinerant career. I will always be grateful to the Department of
Landscape Architecture at that university for the help and en-
couragement it gave me.

The talks became lectures, the lectures expanded into a course,
which was eventually given several years in a row. I touched
on roads and fields, on town and village layouts, on farms and
factories and even places where games were played. I found
myself increasingly interested in the history of those things and
how they helped in the formation of communities. But there
was finally the question of how to describe my topic: what was
the common denominator of all these spaces and structures?
What underlying theory or belief brought them together?
Sometimes it was said that I lectured on "The American Scene,"
or "The American Habitat." Whenever I could, I objected to
the use of the word *environment*. In the sixties, it will be re-
called, the environmental movement was shrill and self-right-
eous, and I had no wish to be identified with it; and this is still
the case. If nevertheless my course was labelled "Studies in the
Man-made environment" (Harvard's phrase) I took pains to say
that neither I nor the course was in any way concerned with

conservation or ecology or the wilderness experience; there was enough important material to cover as it was.

In the end my topic was named "The History of the American Cultural Landscape" — by which was meant the natural environment as modified by man. This was certainly not the best of definitions, but I've not been able to come up with anything better.

The years of teaching were stimulating and agreeable, though they entailed a good deal of work. I learned much that I should have known in the beginning, and learned it from colleagues in geography and history and environmental design and architecture. There was usually enough student support to warrant my going deeper into the subject. Like most laymen I had no conception of the Byzantine complexities of the academic world; it seemed a vast tangle of departments, programs, committees, and struggles for promotion and tenure and fellowships and grants, out of which the initiates skillfully wove lifelong shelters for themselves, but which could only bewilder and frustrate the outsider. I confess it was mortifying to realize that landscape studies, however important to me or acceptable to students, had no claim to academic legitimacy. No doubt it was pleasant for the students to hear about roads and fields and towns, and to see slides (whatever their quality) of filling stations and barns, but where (I was politely asked) did this lead? To which department did it belong, and what did it offer to any graduate program? And who were the recognized authorities in the field and how extensive was the literature? In short *was* there such a thing as landscape studies to which instructors as well as students could dedicate themselves?

These were reasonable questions, and if they no longer disturb me it is because I no longer teach. It remains, I'm afraid, for a younger generation of landscape enthusiasts to solve the important problems of academic accreditation.

But underlying all these questions was one which from the very beginning of my efforts gave me pause: in what way was I making a serious contribution to the students' education? This of course is something every teacher wonders about, and not entirely because his or her job depends on an affirmative answer; and a good teacher, I suppose, is one who designs his or her course so that it prepares the students for a rewarding life. The more I sought some justification for discussing the cultural landscape at such length, the more convinced I was that the course had little practical or scholarly value. So my contribution to the education of my students was simply this: I taught them how to be alert and enthusiastic tourists.

An embarrassing kind of insight! For I was well aware of the low reputation tourists enjoyed all over the world, and in fact I had gone out of my way to denounce the tourist industry as the exploiter and defiler of landscapes. But I was also aware of the fact that what I had tried to share with students was precisely the pleasure and inspiration I myself had acquired not from books, not from college, but from many years of travel. What I was passing on were those experiences as a tourist — or the means of acquiring them — that had been most precious to me.

More than fifty years have passed since I first consulted a Baedeker, and I still look upon almost any guidebook as a book of revelations; I feel a bond with every tourist I see reading the pages of fine print and condensed prose in an effort to interpret the surrounding world. There are obnoxious tourists just as there are obnoxious children, but there is a strong element of snobbery, it seems to me, in our criticism of tourist groups, the condescension of those who belong — who are at home — to those who are strangers without recognizable status. Yet we are all of us strangers, tourists, at one time or another, and from our own experience we should recognize the individual impulse for self-improvement that is back of so much tourist travel. At the risk of exaggerating, I would say that the inspiration of tourism is a desire to know more about the world in order to know more about ourselves. If we offend public taste, that is only incidental to our search; the Swiss cuckoo clock, the bumper-sticker from Carlsbad Caverns is a type of diploma — proof that we have at least *tried* to improve.

Far too much contemporary writing on tourism emphasizes sociological fashion: the problem of increased leisure, conspicuous consumption, the exploitation of impoverished societies, the

power of the tourist industry and so on. What seems to be
overlooked is the educational purpose of most tourism, the long
and valuable educational tradition and the contribution tourism
has made not only to the discovery of the world but to our
way of interpreting it. The rise of tourism some four centuries
ago marked the beginning of a new and much closer relationship between people and the landscape they lived in, and it was
not the philosopher or the scientist who did the pioneering but
the solitary, uninformed traveler, setting out, hardly knowing
why, in search of a new kind of pleasure and a new kind of
knowledge.

If we were to single out any one individual as the father of
tourism I believe Montaigne would be the man. As a traveler
for the sake of travelling he was one of many, but he was
perhaps the first to speculate about why it was that people felt
the urge to leave home to see famous monuments and ancient
cities, and to explore remote regions and observe strange customs. The motive behind travel had changed. It was no longer
the religious incentive, which in the past had inspired many
long and difficult pilgrimages, that drew people to the exploration of new landscapes, and it was no longer the merchant's
search for new markets or new products; it was something
different. As Montaigne defined it, it was the desire to "report
on the temperament of nations and their ways of life," — a
geographical motive. But he also mentioned a motive not
hitherto identified with travel — greater self-awareness; the op-
portunity, Montaigne explained, "to rub our minds and polish
them by contact with others. Traveling through the world produces a marvelous clarity in the judgment of men. We are all
of us confined and enclosed within ourselves, and see no farther
than the end of our nose. This great world is a mirror where
we must see ourselves in order to know ourselves. There are so
many different tempers, so many different points of view, judg-
ments, opinions, laws and customs to teach us to judge wisely
on our own, and to teach our judgment to recognize its im-
perfection and natural weakness."

This notion that minds can be broadened and enriched by
contact with people from different places and different walks of

life accounts at least in part for the importance we now attach to a college education. Knowing the world (as we now understand the phrase) almost always means a kind of intellectual or social awareness, a tolerance of unfamiliar ideas and unfamiliar people; that is why out-of-town Americans subscribe to the *New York Times* — it keeps them abreast, so they like to believe, with what is being said and thought. But to Montaigne and his generation, knowing the world had a richer and more specific meaning: it meant participation in the everyday world of living and working and celebrating. It meant knowing the creations of man, his institutions and art and architecture, and something about the past. Hence the delight felt by early tourists when, after days of rough and dangerous travel, they came to a lively city they had never seen before, and glimpsed a novel ceremony, or conversed with a stranger having something new and amazing to impart. Every scene, every encounter, every landscape taught them something.

They were not as analytical in their observations as we try to be. They generalized very little about the social order they immersed themselves in, and they were rarely critical in matters of art or science. But whenever I have read one of their accounts I have been struck by the sharpness of their sensory response: they describe and comment on the food and wine served at an inn, on the variety of accents, on the instruments played by street musicians, the color and texture of clothes, the smell of crowded rooms, the refreshing sound of fountains, the brilliance of light at a ceremony, the lonely dark of the forest. These sensations had much to do with the way they judged a landscape; and whether we recognize it or not, they still *are* part of our own reaction to a place; only they are not quantifiable, and scholarly descriptions omit them as subjective evidence. Let us hope that the tourists of the future will recapture those sensual pleasures, and record them, for they give an emotional dimension to any landscape and keep its memory alive.

When Montaigne spoke of the world "as a mirror where we must see ourselves in order to know ourselves," he chose his metaphor with care. He meant quite precisely that the face of the earth, the landscape, resembled the face of man. In *The*

Order of Things, Michel Foucault discusses the role which resemblance played in the culture of the 16th Century. "The
universe was folded in upon itself: The earth echoing the sky,
faces seeing themselves reflected in the stars, and plants holding
within their stems the secrets which were of use to man. Painting imitated space. And representation — whether in the service
of pleasure or of knowledge — was posited as a form of repetition: The theater of life or the mirror of nature." [2]

What the world as mirror revealed was clear enough: art, architecture, the hierarchical social order, the order of the cosmos
itself, all reflected the human form, its proportions, the inter-
dependence of its organs and members, its divine origin. Language further emphasized the analogy: one spoke of the head
of state, of the body politic, the arm of the law, the hands working in the fields. It must have been a very satisfactory view of
the world, entirely consistent with Classical tradition, and en-
dorsed by the church; a trustworthy guide to understanding and
accepting human ways. I think we can envy those times when
men and women derived something more substantial than esthetic pleasure from the view of a beautiful and prosperous landscape, when instead of a simple view, they saw the expression of
what seemed an admirable social order, and they gathered evidence that man was still carrying out the divine mandate to
bring nature to perfection. The city, rich and splendid, surrounded by dependent towns and castles and estates, stood as a
central symbol of authority; off in the village fields peasants obe-
diently worked at their assigned tasks, and the whole marvelous
landscape was framed by the distant natural setting.

That early tourist point of view certainly had its shortcom-
ings. It was largely confined to a small though influential class:
men of property and social standing, not much given to looking
beneath the surface of things or to doubting the evidence of
their senses; men having little time for the mysteries of nature
or for speculation about the problems or hopes of obscure and
unimportant people, judging much of the world in terms of
status — boundaries, privileges, wealth and rank. In all these
respects we are probably better than those early tourists. But we
need to remember several things: four hundred years ago the

tourist experience was new and revolutionary; it had only just emerged from an attitude of distrust of the visible world, or at best, indifference to it. However limited their sympathies may have been, the first tourists set out to do what few had ever done before: learn about the world as a means of learning about themselves, and by and large they seem to have succeeded. And finally the manner in which they depicted their adventures, either in art or in writing, was so vivid, so compelling, so revealing of unsuspected beauty and humanity, that subsequent generations accepted their view of the landscape as the only authentic one. It is only within the last decades that we have begun to question the Renaissance canon of landscape beauty, and centuries of blind allegiance are still evident in the layout of our parks and suburbs and even our housing developments and scenic highways. More to the point, tourism is only beginning to throw off the spell of that early discovery and appraisal; to many conscientious tourists the only correct itinerary is still a retracing of the Grand Tour of the 18th Century — the monuments and galleries and ruins and glimpses of sublimity which well-bred young gentlemen of past centuries visited and admired are what many of us continue to visit and admire. As far as knowledge of the world — of a particular aspect of the world — is concerned, a good deal is acquired; today as in the past, travel is broadening, but self-knowledge is something else again. That Renaissance world has long since ceased to be a mirror to modern man: when he looks into it he no longer sees his own image, merely the image of a vanished culture.

How long did this classical form of tourism flourish? Judging from my own experience it was still unchallenged after World War I. Those of my generation (and even older) will remember — with something like uneasiness — how seriously we were schooled in how to perceive the world in the traditional tourist manner. Our initiation called for the knowledge of at least one foreign language — French, German or Italian — and familiarity with an old-fashioned history crowded with names and dates and dynasties, familiarity with an equally old-fashioned geography: boundaries, population, rivers and mountains, leading products. It was scarcely less essential in those days to know something about the principal architectural styles, along with their most famous examples. Required reading for the tourist included Vasari's *Lives of the Painters,* Ruskin's *Stones of Venice,* and a variety of lesser works on European travel and sightseeing, all available in Tauchnitz editions.

Once this background was acquired we were ready to become full-fledged tourists: keeping a diary, carrying a Brownie and a Baedeker and a phrase book, collecting hotel labels and sending picture postcards to envious friends at home. As countless predecessors had done, in every town we dutifully visited the cathedral, the art gallery, the castle, the picturesque medieval quarter. There were carefully planned excursions by boat or streetcar to a nearby suburb to see the celebrated palace, the celebrated garden, the celebrated view. A half century ago the conventional tourist was too much concerned with history to pay attention to contemporary art or politics, though the opera house, provided its repertory was of the familiar sort, was occasionally patronized. The newer parts of town were ignored whenever possible; they contained no *Sehenswürdigkeiten* — objects deserving to be seen.

The present generation may well feel nothing but scorn for this type of orthodox tourism with its blind veneration of the antique, its avoidance of the unexpected, its dogged pursuit of culture. Even in its heyday it was laughed at, and a stock figure on the stage and in cartoons was the indefatigable tourist, usually German, studying every inscription and every ruin. Education was the incentive, rather than self-knowledge, and I think it would be easy to relate fashions in tourist attitudes and objectives to prevailing educational theories; Baedeker, both in style and content, has much in common with the 19th Century Ph.D. dissertation on art history.

One reason we have such a low opinion of pre–World War II tourists is that we associate them with luxurious trans-Atlantic liners, expensive hotels and resorts where they hobnobbed with Russian grand dukes and English lords. But the fact of the matter is, few of us had much money to spend. Travel across the ocean meant ten days in a crowded cabin, travel in Europe meant third class in trains, austere little hotels or pensions with one bath to the floor, and often very meager fare: an orange or a pear for dessert. In those days before all-expense group tours and low cost tourist accommodations, tourists had to shift for themselves and were forever on the lookout for cheap excursion fares, seats in the third balcony, and such free entertainments as public concerts in the park, the evening corso or promenade, and the newspapers available in the cafés. Being a tourist meant being an outsider, an inexperienced member of the public. Isolated from the commonplace world by tour buses and guides, the modern tourist is protected from foreign-ness, but in the old days we wanted to pass as natives, if only to avoid being overcharged by street vendors and taxi drivers. I'm inclined to believe that this urge to be assimilated, combined with our incessant search for the famous landmarks, had the effect of making us highly conscious of local characteristics and allowed us to develop an awareness of the peculiarities of a place and its inhabitants, and to compare them with those of other places — a constant topic of discussion in the pastry shops frequented by tourists.

It was, to be sure, a cautious, uneventful, and at times a fatiguing and solitary way of passing a summer vacation: tramping out to admire Baedeker's list of three-star monuments, conscientiously sampling the local food, taking lessons in conversational French or German or Italian, and always trying not to resemble a tourist. But as I look back on many summers of such European travel I wonder if they were not in fact an excellent introduction to the different phase of tourism that I have learned to call landscape studies. Art-historical names, dates, and facts were eventually forgotten, but art in its much less monumental guise, and history as memory of events, confronted me — so I found — in every street name, every roof, every accent. Sooner or later this happens to every dedicated tourist: he ventures beyond the guidebook itinerary and discovers that the workaday surrounding world reminds him of the art-historical world of the gallery; he looks out of the train window and discovers to his surprise that the countryside shares many of the traits of the city — the parish church, the layout of the fields, the glare of the sun in a village street are recognizable variations on their city

counterparts; city and country belong together in a unique landscape, and this newly discovered entity seems far older, far more
venerable than the oldest monument.

It would be too much to say that all tourists responded to this
glimpse of a broader, less familiar horizon. The old tradition
died hard, and most travelers relied on the art-historical guidebook to tell them what to admire and where to go. Food and
accommodations in out-of-the-way villages were likely to be
bad, and the natives were rarely cordial. Still, in the years between the wars a change was gradually taking place in public
attitudes toward the back country, and the more adventurous
tourist learned to wander farther afield.

The increase in the number of automobiles had much to do
with the change, and social legislation providing for paid vaca-
tions brought city workers and employees to parts of the country where life was cheap. But no young American, fresh out of
college as I was, could have failed to be aware that part of the
social ferment in Europe was a general reappraisal of almost
every aspect of the environment, urban as well as rural. Cities
were expanding; new housing, new streets, new recreation
areas, new suburbs were threatening to obliterate the traditional
composition. Attempts to modernize agriculture, to improve
farm and village living, along with the need to create jobs and
provide for tourists, alerted many people to the condition of the
countryside. The national or regional landscape — its development or preservation — became a topic of heated debate. Along
with countless exhibits, photo displays, museums devoted to
folklore and rural history, there was violent denunciation —
with political overtones, especially in central Europe — of the
inroads of industrialization and urbanization and the depravity
of "modern" architecture. In every country the argument was
loud and exciting, and for my part I can only say that I found
the romanticizing of the traditional landscape sympathetic to
my way of seeing the world. How could it have been otherwise? It was precisely that aspect of the landscape I had been
taught to admire that was being threatened: the vestiges of an
old, pre-industrial, pre-democratic order, the fragments of a way
of life that had been described and praised by great names in

literature and art for more than four centuries. There could be
no other civilization than this. And what confirmed my love of
the established landscape was the tendency — by no means confined to politically reactionary elements — to analyze landscapes
not simply as the haphazard products of economic or environmental forces but as profound expressions of ethnic or racial
traits. The ancestral landscape created a special breed of men
and women with common psychological and physical characteristics, and this came about through centuries-old attachment to
the land; it was only by being rooted in the land, by having a
peasant or land-holding background, by having undergone the
ineffable influences of a certain climate, a certain topography,
that a true German or Englishman or Frenchman came into
being. It followed that a landscape was a cultural heritage that
must at all costs be preserved intact.

This view is no longer widely held. While it lasted it did
enormous damage, yet it also opened our eyes to the variety
surrounding us and the unsuspected wealth of vernacular culture which every nation contained. We learned to see a great
deal we had previously ignored. I think there never was a time
when I found the traditional European landscape more satisfying, more beautiful, more inspiring, than in those final summers
before World War II. The ancient city silhouettes were still un-
disturbed by highrise buildings, there were no massive industrial complexes in the countryside. There was little traffic; tourist resorts were elegant and small, and every view was close to
perfection, as if God's mandate had almost been fulfilled and
man was nearing the end of his labors.

My last prolonged experience of the European landscape came
during World War II when I was in combat intelligence. Much
of the ground covered by the unit I was part of was familiar to
me from the recent past, but I grew to know it in greater detail
and in a more practical way in the course of trying to find out
the topographical characteristics and the significant human features of the area immediately in front of us. The landscape we
fought over during the last winter of the war was heavily industrialized, criss-crossed by rail lines and highways and canals,
with many factories and mines, and factory towns containing

long rows of workers' houses, each with a small vegetable garden. In normal times I suppose the streets would have been crowded with men and women going to work on bicycles or in streetcars, and coal smoke would have floated from the tall chimneys. The towns were not old; except for an occasional half-timbered farm house, unaccountably wedged in at an angle among the modern buildings, they had nothing picturesque or historical to show. Much of the time the sky was overcast, and it rained or snowed a great deal.

Bombing and artillery fire soon reduced the towns to ruins. The streets were choked with rubble, and what there was of open country showed mile after mile of sagging powerlines. Everywhere there were craters full of black water that trembled after an explosion.

Armies do more than destroy, they create an order of their own. It was strange to observe how both sides superimposed a military landscape on the landscape of devastation. It was even more strange, I thought, to see how the military landscape resembled the old pre-technological landscape, especially in the way it organized space. This was most apparent in studying a map, either one of our own or one captured from the enemy. The traditional spatial order reappeared, though in a contemporary form: the centers of authority and power were heavily circled in red crayon and marked with those heraldic devices which the military use to indicate a specific administrative status — headquarters, command post, supply depot. Surrounding the important centers were the subordinate centers — feudal dependencies, so to speak — with their own heraldic devices. A great web of boundaries divided the countryside into innumerable sectors, and a system of different colors and different kinds of lines showed where each belonged in the hierarchy of spaces. As in the ancient European landscape, these territorial divisions were of great significance, and when we got hold of an enemy map showing a change in the boundaries or in their occupants we sought to deduce what this meant in the way of a tactical decision — much as in the old days it might have signified a new and dangerous dynastic alliance.

The civilian population had almost entirely disappeared, but

it had been replaced by another, very different one: thousands
of highly disciplined men, each of them doing what he was
trained to do, going where he was told, eating what he was fed.
Many of them camped out in the half-ruined, rainsoaked homes
of the workers — impoverished houses smelling of wet clothing
and patent medicines and rotting potatoes. The men identified
themselves not by where they lived but by who their leader was.
They rarely knew the name of the town, and when out of touch
with their unit, they felt lost. It was a way of seeing themselves
that they grew accustomed to, and they were hostile to the lead-
erless groups of refugees and looters and deserters that moved
freely from ruin to ruin, or hid in the woods.

Pageantry is scarcely the word to use, but it comes to mind
when I recall the display of signs and notices that covered almost every lamp post and tree in the military landscape. The
signs were often large and striking, composed of symbols and
acronyms and colors, which had to be deciphered before they
could be understood. Code names for units, drawn from mythol-
ogy or comic strip characters, were inscribed on directional
arrows: "Wieland," "Mickey Mouse," "Gasoline Alley Four,"
"Walhalla West." Bedraggled flags and pennants, lengths of
colored wire and tape festooned the fences and the walls of
houses like remnants of a bygone carnival, a medieval holiday,
perhaps, where everyone appeared in the costume of his trade
or craft. And in fact the military landscape was a place where
dress, as in the old days, had great symbolic meaning. No matter how dirty or tattered a uniform might be, it revealed by
means of a shoulder patch, a stripe, an epaulette, many details
about a man: his special skill, the unit he belonged to, and his
rank; it was not necessary to know more.

All these signs and symbols to provide information or to establish relationships were a novelty to us; previously we had
been private individuals, finding our own way. But I believe
that on the whole we liked the pervasive symbolism. Symbols
of course had been common in earlier times when few persons
knew how to read; they had told the public much that it had to
know. In the military landscape they served an added purpose:
they reminded us that we were part of an immense organiza-

tion, that by being able to decipher them we proved that we had
been initiated into a group secret, that we were bona fide members of the military society.

They also introduced us to the complexity and extent of the
organization, the political dimension of the landscape, as it
were. Informational symbols were especially numerous wherever there were men not familiar with the locality: at crossroads
or places of assembly or at a headquarters. In the military landscape it always seemed to me that the important headquarters,
even when concealed in a forest or a ruined manor house,
played the role once played by the city — the focal point of
power and knowledge and display, a place where everyone
wanted to be. I never visited such a headquarters without thinking of its resemblance to the Renaissance cities old travelers had
described. There was the same profusion of important public
buildings next to one another (tents with signs in front of them
and a guard); the same profusion of insignia — on staff officers,
clerks, MPs; the same important men to be glimpsed. A spot-
less jeep arrived with a celebrated battalion commander, spic-
and-span in a clean uniform but resolutely macho with his
carbine, and hand grenades taped to his combat jacket, and his
shiny combat boots. There ensued a rigidly correct exchange
of salutes. Everyone, performers and spectators alike, enjoyed the
display of military etiquette. The Field of the Cloth of Gold had
many imitations on the fields of olive-drab. The Renaissance
still flourished in combat headquarters; that was where the
decorated heroes were to be found, and where there were
ceremonies. It was in fact the 16th Century military engineer
who helped give the city its modern form. He not only fortified
it, he devised the grid of rectangular spaces to accommodate
the various military units according to their standing in the
social hierarchy of the times, and he placed a square in the
center for drills and parades — a design still used in every army
encampment, and in almost every modern town.

Surrounding the headquarters there was a different and much
larger element of the military landscape, and for a time I liked
to believe that it too had its Renaissance counterpart: that it
represented the countryside with villages inhabited by peasants

ruled by a local lord. At the end of increasingly bad and dangerous roads, located in a remote farmhouse or railroad station
or in the basement of a ruined factory — in any case near to
the enemy — were scattered the combat units, companies and
batteries and platoons, all of them much more aware of the
military landscape as an environment than as a social entity.
The men in those places led a much less formal existence; communication between them was based less on the symbol and
the written word than on gesture and voice. Insignia of rank
were inconspicuous and less necessary. Even the map, too small
in scale, too lacking in detail for the use of men on foot, played
a minor role. It was a more pragmatic way of life, and the
young and often inexperienced officers usually shared quarters
and food and leisure with the men. Occasionally such units
found themselves living comfortably and well, but most of the
time their shelter was primitive and makeshift.

What really distinguished these men from their colleagues
at headquarters was their greater awareness of the environment.
If the men at headquarters led an urban existence, what kind
of existence was that of the men in the companies and platoons?
One could hardly call it rural; most of the time they were in
built-up areas, though those in the country sometimes killed a
deer or made off with a chicken. Perhaps we can say they were
part-time hunters, not in the obvious sense that they were hunters
of men, but in the sense that hunters develop an acute receptivity
to the messages sent out by the environment. In a very short time
the men learned to rely on their senses for guidance; whether they
were in a town or in the open country, their senses constantly
picked up information — the smell of cordite, the smell of dead
bodies, even the smell of the enemy, for each army had a
characteristic body odor. There were the sounds of different
kinds of gunfire, the sound of shells flying overhead; the sound
of footsteps, the sound of vehicles. On comparatively silent
nights men on patrol learned to listen for the sound of ration
trucks bringing food to the enemy, miles away. Any bright or
sudden light was enough to rouse the soundest sleeper.

In peacetime, weather and topography — to say nothing of the
texture of the soil and the density of the foliage — were never

looked upon as of much consequence, but in the outlying units, always aware of the night patrols ahead of them, and of the need for supplies, they were sometimes inflated into matters of life and death. Even the phases of the moon were worried about.

In itself there was nothing unusual about this environmental awareness. Experience promptly showed how essential it was, and every man took pains to cultivate it. What made it immensely valuable was that it was a *shared* experience, talked about, passed on to newcomers, and accepted by all as part of their combat existence. It had little in common with a feeling for nature, and indeed it derived more from urban than from country hazards. These sensory responses were rarely of an exalted kind: loathing of the taste of C rations, the luxurious feel of clean clothes, the warmth and light of a roadside fire — all those hands stretching out of the darkness toward the flames! — their joy at the coming of sunny days in the spring; these were simply commonplace ways of participating in the world through the senses, but sharing them, recognizing them in others, made men remember their humanity. Even now, a generation later, some of them still discover that a certain smell, a certain taste, a certain kind of early morning overcast sky can bring back a mood, an event, a landscape from the past as if it had been yesterday.

This is how we should think of landscapes: not merely how they look, how they conform to an esthetic ideal, but how they satisfy elementary needs: the need for sharing some of those sensory experiences in a familiar place: popular songs, popular dishes, a special kind of weather supposedly found nowhere else, a special kind of sport or game, played only here in this spot. These things remind us that we belong — or used to belong — to a specific place: a country, a town, a neighborhood. A landscape should establish bonds between people, the bond of language, of manners, of the same kind of work and leisure, and above all a landscape should contain the kind of spatial organization which fosters such experiences and relationships; spaces for coming together, to celebrate, spaces for solitude, spaces that never change and are always as memory depicted them. These are some of the characteristics that give a landscape its uniqueness, that give it style. These are what make us recall it with emotion.

Not necessarily agreeable emotion: the military landscape provided us with a spatial order dedicated to sudden and violent movement, a set of relationships based on total subordination and anonymity, and a sensory experience based on death and the premonition of death; it was the ugly caricature of a landscape. Nevertheless, it functioned, and even its horrors instructed us in what a good landscape, and a good social order, should be.

I doubt if I can ever again contemplate the Classical European landscape and its American variations — or for that matter any other landscape — exclusively from the objective, art-historical point of view. It is not that I can no longer appreciate its beauty, and it is certainly not that I suppose we are capable of ever producing a similar harmony between men and their environment. Perhaps it is because I think the day is past when harmony, adjustments, can be our landscape criterion; what we contemporary men and women are, and what we are becoming is something which can no longer be faithfully reflected in the visible landscape. For the military landscape revealed two aspects of humanity: it was not only a throwback to the brutality and primitiveness of the Dark Ages, it was also a glimpse of the future. Those urgent, unremitting efforts to establish communications, the trailing wires and signs and symbols and colored lights, foreshadowed our present groping for new kinds of community. That overreaching lust for power and mobility and final solutions is still transforming and mutilating the environment. The search for sensory experiences of the world as the most reliable source of self-knowledge is more insistent than ever.

Landscapes showing those characteristics are becoming numerous, and I think that is why we are increasingly fascinated by immense cities, industrialized regions, the desert, the wilderness, and with parts of the world awash with new and migrating populations. We seem to be living in the midst of a second and more massive *völkerwanderung,* in a period when old landscapes disappear and new landscapes involving new relationships, new demands on the environment are slowly taking form. And as I see it, it is in those places where what we call landscape studies can be particularly rewarding.

Yet I myself cannot entirely forget my tourist past; I still prefer the landscapes I have known and where I can at least partly understand the expressions of cultural values. History, or a dependence on history, is still essential, even though it is a history which treats the vernacular and the everyday event. Art also belongs with landscape studies as I interpret them, for it is only when we begin to participate emotionally in a landscape that its uniqueness and beauty are revealed to us.

Nearer than Eden

HOW CAN WE POSSIBLY READ — or even keep count of — all the books published in the past few years in praise of the garden! Not every one is a picture book; there are small pocket-sized anthologies of garden-verse, and collections of letters, and intimate glimpses of gardens in other parts of the world and at other times. There are ecological treatises, and eloquent accounts of what gardening means to modern man. There are calendars of gardens, handbooks on gardening, TV programs on how to plant a garden, and guided tours of private gardens. In the supermarket — the garden's modern day successor at least in terms of produce — we can buy garden magazines and tapes of seeds with directions on how to make a garden of our own. If anything, there is *too* much garden literature available; it is often repetitious, has too much to say about the spiritual benefits of gardening, contains too many art photographs of flowers, too many italicized quotations from Thoreau. But still, as enthusiasms go, it would be hard to find one more innocent, more generous, more appealing than this contemporary love of the garden.

It is appealing because it resembles a springtime flowering — and a time of bumper harvests for the lucky publishers and photographers; yet like any springtime it has occurred with dependable regularity throughout history. An immense amount of art and literature has always been devoted to the celebration of the garden — as art, as symbol, as source of delight. The garden has always been an object of love and even a degree of veneration. It is easy to understand why; but one reason for the present outpouring of interest, I believe, is that the garden represents an archetype — one of those images which, along with the dwelling and the road and the shrine, are seen as essential elements in any desirable landscape. Without the garden, the landscape, even the imaginary landscape, is incomplete. As we now visualize it, the garden stands for a particular kind of experience of the environment, essential to a fuller understanding of ourselves: the garden is where we *have* to be. It is precisely now, when urban existence makes it all but impossible for most of us to relish the quality of a space, when any contact with a garden in particular is out of the question, that the search for the archetype, a rediscovery and confirmation of its existence, becomes so urgent. Hence the flood of books.

Yet unhappily the fact is that our knowledge of gardens and gardening is more and more limited to what is a literary or (at best) a spectator experience, to someone else's interpretation. Circumstances oblige us to accept the garden at second-hand, to accept the image without perceiving anything of the archetypal garden itself. Like the dwelling the garden has no single, universally accepted form; like the dwelling it is much more than the product of a design or of evironmental influences, and like the dwelling it serves many needs and is thought of in many ways. We can in fact say that precisely because *it is* an archetype the garden must be subject to constant reinterpretation; there are as many kinds of gardens as there are concepts of art and work and community, and of relationships to the natural world. Even within a given culture there are many versions of the garden. Yet we somehow recognize them all.

It is therefore only by examining some of these versions that we can arrive at a clearer understanding of what the garden really signifies, and why we value it so highly. The role of the garden in our own Western culture, going back in history as far as we can, will serve as an example. There are surprises, suggestions of a deeper significance, even in the origin of the word itself. "Garden" comes from an Indo-European root, *gher,* which appears in many Latin and Greek and Slavic and Germanic words for such apparently disparate things as farmyard, pasture, sown field, hedge, house, fence, enclosure, stable, girder, fortified place — and garden. All these words clearly imply enclosure or an enclosed space, and in modern German *Garten* seems to indicate less what our dictionaries define as "a plot of land used for the cultivation of flowers, vegetables, and fruit" than it does an enclosure or container; so that Germans speak of tree-gardens and animal-gardens and wine-gardens and even sometimes of corpse-gardens, while in English we either use a distinct term such as orchard or zoo or day-nursery, or use a term compounded with a word meaning enclosure: dog-pound, sheep-run, bull-pen, chicken-yard, and so on. We are determined to see the garden in terms of vegetation, and that may be one of our problems.

For as a matter of fact the earliest gardens in our history were essentially enclosures, built for defense or privacy or storage or for growing food. If we look back several thousand years to a time when wandering groups of people started to appear in Europe out of Asia, we can try to visualize one such band of men and women and children, some on foot, some on horseback, some in wagons, slowly herding their cows and pigs and sheep. Finally they decided to settle down in a place with a sufficiency of grass and water and firewood, where the soil was not too heavy for their small wooden plows and where there was protection against sudden attack. The various families or households built themselves crude, round huts out of reeds and mud and wood. "Gradually," a historian writes, "each individual household, having settled in a certain spot, would build a fenced or hedged enclosure around their farmyard, *hortus,* for a dwelling, storehouse, and barnyard. This then became the locus of, and an adjunct to that household. It was put to permanent use by this group and so identified itself with them as a permanent site." [1] *Hortus* derives from *gher,* and one is struck by the fact that the concept of garden was, in the early days, closely involved with the concepts of family or household, of property, of defense, and even of community layout, and though the word becomes more closely identified in the course of centuries with the growing of plants, we can never entirely divorce the garden from its social meaning; when we do so, we run the risk of defining the garden in strictly esthetic or ecological terms — which is what many people are doing now.

If we try to visualize those primitive enclosures, those first attempts to organize space on a permanent basis, we see few resemblances to the modern garden. The enclosures, even at the beginning, varied considerably in size, depending not only on the number of people in the family, but also on its prestige. As the community grew in population and density, many of the enclosures were subdivided, and though at first they were roughly oval or round in shape they eventually assumed rectangular form: narrow on the street or alley side, but stretching in length. All of them were essentially homesteads, headquarters for extended families, symbolically and legally important as visible evidence that the household was part of the community with a permanent claim on a piece of land. And it is necessary to bear in mind that in addition to the enclosure each family had the use of farmland, located somewhere outside the village, where they raised field-crops — barley and oats and a kind of wheat, and in addition to the farmland, each family in good standing was entitled to graze its livestock in the village pasture.

So the enclosure served as a place of residence, a place of storage, and on occasion a place of defense. We find this division in holdings in many pre-industrial societies: dwellings clustered in a village, farmlands somewhere outside. A good deal depended on what the farmlands raised by way of food: with the Pueblo Indians, for instance, their farmlands (often called gardens because of the way they were cultivated) provided almost all the food the family consumed — corn and beans and squash. But in most of Europe in the Dark Ages, and even in the Middle Ages, the farmland provided grains and not much else. It was necessary to supplement the grains, both by raising livestock and by exploiting the forest resources: by hunting wild berries and fruits and herbs. Nevertheless a more reliable and more convenient source of vegetables was desirable, and this was where the garden in the horticultural sense came into the picture: the enclosure was where certain fruits and vegetables were grown, strictly for the needs of the family — or various branches of the family, for the enclosure usually accommodated a collection of sons and daughters and cousins and dependents — with separate huts, but feeling a common identity and loyalty to the head of the family.

The enclosure had the appearance of a primitive, somewhat disorderly, farmyard: with chickens and geese, an occasional sick cow or cow and calf, an occasional sheep, an occasional pig or two to consume whatever garbage there was. The pigs eventually provided the family with meat and lard. There were small beds of those vegetables which needed frequent attention and were part of the daily diet: lentils, cabbage, onions, turnips and others, beds of herbs, either for flavoring or for medicine — parsley, mustard, chives, sage, dill, and possibly marjoram and basil. Somewhere in the enclosure was likely to be a beehive, and almost always a stand of fruit and nut trees. Flowers were rare and were grown either for medicinal purposes or for good luck.

Nowhere in this enclosure was there any evidence of taste or feeling for beauty: mud, weeds, filth were everywhere. Yet if we look hard enough and close enough we can discern a definite order which in the course of the centuries was formalized and became characteristic of the traditional garden and even of the large and pretentious pleasure garden of the Renaissance.

The enclosure itself, the fence or hedge surrounding the area, was the most conspicuous element of the composition. Made out of brush and vines, plastered with mud, painstakingly woven out of reeds and stalks and branches, it was an effective barrier, keeping out foxes and wolves and stray cattle, discouraging any trespassing or theft, its height and sturdiness and repair regulated by law: there could be no garden, legally speaking, without a hedge or wall or fence; there could be no legal protection for the life and property of the family unless it built such a hedge or fence or wall; there could be no guarantee of privacy, no self-rule by the family unless that boundary was established, made visible, and carefully maintained. Our own fence laws, inherited from England, are essentially the same as those which prevailed in medieval Europe.

The focus of the enclosure was of course the dwelling, the permanent structure which succeeded the temporary hut or col-

lection of huts. Without going into the legal status of the
dwelling, it should be pointed out that a characteristic of our
Western garden is the close association between it and the
dwelling: "house and garden," "toft and croft," are familiar
phrases indicating how the two elements developed together in
our culture; and this is not merely a spatial relationship, for
the whole enclosure was loosely organized around the dwelling.
The vegetable and herb plots were next to the house, because
by tradition the woman of the house tended them and used
them. Beyond this kitchen garden, in the rear of the enclosure,
stood the orchard with its own fence or hedge. There is evidence that the orchard was the first area to be recognized as a
garden in our modern use of the word, the first area within the
enclosure to be permanently transformed and to be given legal
status and protection — not only because of the utilitarian value
of its fruit and nut trees, but because of its use as a place of
assembly. The orchard, as part of the larger enclosures belong-
ing to a prince or king, was the scene of receptions and important ceremonies, and on the village level it was often where
the public gathered for celebrations. When the history of the
common garden is written I suspect we will discover that the
village orchard was the early forerunner of the park; in central
Europe the orchard is still a favorite place for holiday gatherings and even political rallies.

The garden or enclosure was thus long defined as a distinct
family-centered, family-ruled territory, withdrawn or detached
from the village community, not only in the eyes of its occupants but in the eyes of the law. Once the hedge or fence was
erected, the authorities recognized its autonomy: whoever invaded a garden, by climbing a fence or destroying it, could be
punished by the aggrieved landowner. The symbolic sanctity of
the fence was further shown by the ancient custom which
allowed a convicted criminal, whose house was confiscated as
a penalty, to escape all further punishment by vaulting over his
fence and leaving the village. The length of the vaulting pole
was prescribed. The garden, but not necessarily the house, was
frequently exempt from being tithed. What in German were
called *Gartenrecht* or garden rights were naturally much sought

after.[2] Garden rights were given by the village authorities to
homesteads within the enclosed area of the village; such rights
meant that the land in question had to be completely surrounded by a fence. It was then considered a relatively autonomous area. In the case of ancient holdings a garden right
was automatic, but as the horticultural aspect of the garden
became more important, when the garden began to play a larger
role in the production of food, the demand for the legal status
became more general, and for a very good reason: the legally
recognized garden was exempt from the land use regulations of
the village. In other words the garden was identified not only
as a territory, a family possession, but later as an economic unit
with its own approach to work and the organization of work.

Until about three centuries ago most villages in England,
northern France, Germany, and Scandinavia practiced a kind of
collective farming. The agricultural lands were usually divided into three, sometimes four, large *fields,* in each of which
each qualified villager had a piece of land. Each field was
plowed in the spring by all the concerned landholders acting
cooperatively: it was then planted to one crop, and in the
autumn harvested, again cooperatively. The next year each field
was again plowed, but sown to a different crop. The third
year it was allowed to lie fallow, and the village cattle were
turned loose to graze on the stubble and weeds. The order of
this lying fallow rotated, so that any one year a third — or a
fourth — of the village lands bore no crops. In the absence of an
abundant supply of fertilizer this three (or four) field system
of rotation was the only way to restore the fertility of the soil
and at the same time provide feed of a sort for the livestock.

The crops which each man produced on his pieces of land,
as well as his share of the livestock, belonged to him and his
family. But the crops he planted, the dates when he plowed and
harvested and when the cattle were turned into the empty
fields, were decided by the village authorities and varied little
from year to year or for that matter from decade to decade. It
was an ingenious and relatively fair system; if no one could
choose which plants he wanted to grow, if no one could experiment or operate independently from his neighbors, no one was

likely to starve. Farming was a strictly disciplined, highly conservative undertaking, and once a man was familiar with it he was not likely to be taken by surprise or be confronted by a problem which was new; all could help one another, and did so. And by the same token, changes and innovations were not welcome. New crops, new tools, new methods were resisted, not simply out of conservatism but because they often threatened to disorganize the layout of the fields, alter the farming calendar, and in general raise havoc with a highly organized work system of interlocking, interdependent roles.

The garden, even the medieval peasant garden, possessed an entirely different set of values. It is not easy to put one's finger on the basic distinction between field and garden in our Western landscape. It is not essentially a matter of size or even of tools, for there are many kinds of farms just as there are many kinds of gardens. The current dictionary definition of a farm is of no help: "A tract of agricultural land together with the fields, buildings, animals and personnel there assembled for the purpose of producing a crop or crops."

I believe that we will reach a more useful distinction between the two, at least in traditional terms, when we consider the relation of each to the dwelling and the family. The true garden was next to the house, almost an extension of it; the wife was as much involved in its planting and care as was the man; furthermore all members of the family worked in it, and its produce was exclusively for the household. The medieval farm, even when surrounding the dwelling, was essentially the domain of the man.

Another, more visible distinction between them was the type of work each required. The garden, no matter what its size, called for incessant, detailed, diversified work — a series of small chores, many of them demanding skill and judgment. Since the garden — even the medieval garden — contained a variety of plants, some of them novelties, it could not be adequately taken care of in a routine or perfunctory manner; each plant, each vine, each tree had to be put in the ground, cultivated, pruned, grafted, watered, transplanted, and harvested in a special way and at a special moment, and all this was done by hand or by the use of small and simple tools — hoe and spade and knife.

A final distinction: the garden was always based on a systematic intervention in the natural order, on the creation of an artificial environment. The weather was modified by protection against wind and sun and frost, water was provided, the soil enriched, and the plant itself was altered in shape and size and time of maturity, and eventually it became the creation of the gardener, unable to survive without his or her care.

Is it necessary to contrast this kind of work with that of the traditional worker in the field? The neat rows of seeds, carefully distinguished, and the seeds thrown by the handful over the rough plowland; the careful succession of small duties in the garden throughout the growing season, and the periods of intense work of the farmer in the spring and again in the fall alternating with periods of inactivity, long weeks when the crops are not yet harvested, long months when the fields lie fallow?

The difference between the two points of view, between the two landscapes, has always been recognized; the field was the man's domain, the garden the woman's; one stretching to the forest and even invading it, the other confined to the surroundings of the dwelling. Historically speaking, it was only in the 15th Century that a confrontation developed. The rise of the garden to a position of prominence and prestige, its achievement of a fuller definition, came about in two distinct ways: with the growth of the cities and the development of a market for garden produce, and with the growth of a scientific interest in botany and the consequent introduction of many new plants. These were not always garden plants, but the garden has always been more hospitable to novelties than the field, if only because the introduction of a new vegetable, a new herb, a new tree rarely entails a drastic reorganization of space or routine, or a need for new equipment; and the mentality of the gardener is more receptive.

The history of 17th Century Virginia illustrates the point. When no gold was found, no route to the Orient was discovered, the Virginia Company decided that the future pros-

perity of the Colony lay in agriculture. In consequence a variety
of tropical plants — oranges, figs, lemons, pineapples, cotton,
tobacco — were imported from elsewhere in America. They
were then distributed to settlers having gardens, men and
women likely to know how to give them individual attention.
Unfortunately there was also the climate to contend with, and
few of the exotic imports survived for more than a year.

Much the same procedure was followed in Europe; new
plants — vegetables, grasses, herbs, trees — underwent their ac-
climatization in botanical gardens or in the gardens of rich
amateurs, but eventually they appeared in the gardens of landowners and even of peasants: asparagus, artichokes, cauliflower,
as well as corn and tobacco and potatoes, were being widely
raised in the last years of the 16th Century. A consequence of
the greater variety of garden plants and of the more efficient
methods used in cultivating them was an increase in the size
and number of gardens. Truck gardens and market gardens
were a common feature of the suburban landscape of many
European cities: near London in the early years of the 17th
Century "a large amount of enclosed land facilitated the
development of individual practices and an intensified commercial agriculture," [3] and the Dutch landscape was in many
suburban regions devoted to the commercial raising of herbs,
vegetables, and flowers. Even more remarkable was the growth
and expansion of home gardens in villages and small towns.
In central Europe the privilege of a garden right on vacant land
within the village itself was much sought after, and it became
common to grant such a right even in the open fields near
the village: a small plot of land would be temporarily fenced
and planted to garden vegetables, then when plowing time or
harvesting or grazing time came the fence would be removed, and the land would revert to the customary collective
exploitation. But more and more garden rights were granted
on a permanent basis, and for all the protests and complaints of
farmers, the uniform expanse of the village's fields was interrupted, first by rows of fruit trees clinging to the roads and
lanes and boundaries and then by full-fledged orchards, and
gardens devoted to strawberries or green peas or lettuce.

Perhaps we should think of those extramural gardens as mere extensions or annexes of the gardens in the village: different in location but similar in function. The *real* landscape revolution came somewhat later, when the techniques of gardening were applied wholesale to the crops in the field, when for the first time the fields were planted to new crops and tended in a new way. No one knows when the experiment was first tried, but by mid–17th Century, carrots were being grown in England as field crops, and so were turnips and cabbages, and the potato was a field crop by the end of the century. This taking over of the field by garden crops and gardening tech-. niques is what the French agrarian historian, Marc Bloch, has called the triumph of horticulture over farming. "It saw the invasion of the arable by garden produce, garden methods (weeding and intensive manuring) and garden conditions (no free grazing, and fencing where necessary)." [4]

So plants which had hitherto always grown in garden beds near the house, always under the eye of the family — hemp, flax, clover, tobacco, potatoes, corn, and sometimes wheat — were graduated to the open field and left to the mercy of the field workers.

This was one of those 17th Century developments which ended by changing not only the ancient feudal order of society and of work on the continental landscape, but the landscape itself. The horiticultural triumph did not proceed everywhere at the same pace; the Enclosure Movement in 16th Century England anticipated it, except then it was not garden plants that were introduced into the field, but livestock, especially sheep; and parts of Europe — not always the most backward — clung to the old order until well into the 19th Century. Just the same, a radical shift was taking place. We know very little about the various stages in the change. When did a farm village first realize that the old routine of collective plowing, planting, and harvesting no longer worked? When did the peasant, used to being able to take a hand in every operation, first see that there were jobs he could not do and crops he could not take care of? And when did people learn to perceive the new landscape and appraise its beauty and usefulness in different terms?

We could deduce something like answers from studying the many books about gardening and farming that started to appear in the 16th Century. Although they had little to say about flowers they gave much attention to every phase of gardening: herb garden, kitchen garden, orchard, and pleasure garden. The garden had acquired a very important role. It had not only become the nursery for new plants and new techniques, it had become a small center for study and experimentation — for satisfying the curiosity everyone felt about botany and its secrets. And most significantly, the garden was being perceived as a work of art. By the end of the 16th Century, French and Italian garden books, many of them translated into English, were offering plans for the layout of gardens. To be sure, the gardens they discussed were usually those of country noblemen or persons of wealth, and the designs were intended not merely to produce beauty but a way of classifying plants. But the effect of all this thought was to give the garden a new prestige, and a new charm.

The history of the garden during those two centuries can be interpreted, it seems to me, as a gradual redefinition. The garden had been an enclosed domestic domain; it had been a source of food and materials and a place of family solidarity in work. Now it became something much richer: a source of stimulation and knowledge and shared delight. The greater familiarity with the nature and origin of plants and trees, with their varieties and characteristics, provided intellectual fare. And at the same time it revealed to the reverent layman some of the laws governing the universe. The garden became an almost sacred place; its seclusion and beauty, and the innocent sociability and work it provided, reminded many of earlier legendary gardens. It is impossible to open a volume from this period that deals with farming and gardening without discovering references to Paradise and the Garden of Eden; to Solomon and Cyrus and Homer and Virgil, and to the joys of helping God perfect Creation. The garden, we are assured, is the perfect setting for domestic harmony, for health, for educating the child, and for forgetting the vexations of the world.

But how about farming? If the garden produced such edifying results what was wrong with the farm? Why were the peasants working in the field not equally blessed? Because Classical tradition still assigned them the lowest place in the social order — because, in the words of a medieval prelate, "They are anxious only for this present life, like brute beasts, and care not for God." [5] The ruinous wars of the 16th and 17th Centuries kept much of continental Europe in a condition of poverty and ignorance; government restrictions on trade, the maze of customs barriers, the bad roads all prevented the rural population from benefiting from scientific and technological innovations. In the 17th Century European landscape the garden stood out as an island of peaceful beauty, a miniature social order, an archetype deriving from history and myth.

Why did this particular vision of the perfect garden not last? Why did it begin to fade in the 18th Century and then entirely disappear from the average homestead? Practical, economic reasons are the easiest to supply. Industrialization, even in its earliest stage, made many garden products superfluous or obsolete: textiles and dyes and medicines, even prepared foods, came to the village from mills and factories and from overseas; many rural families were attracted to the cities, and those who remained in the country found it advantageous to shift their gardening from self-sufficiency to commercialized specialization. Applied botany lost interest in the garden and in the needs of the traditional consumer and preferred to cater to industry and to the commercial farmer; plants were developed and improved and introduced directly to the field, bypassing the garden and isolating it from change. Mechanization came in the 19th Century, and further handicapped the gardener who remained loyal to more painstaking methods.

To these explanations might be added the intellectual change which became general in the 18th Century and which altered our way of understanding the order of creation. It could in fact be said that the time came when we were no longer entirely satisfied with the traditional botanical approach, its emphasis on minute description and its almost medieval concern for precise classification, its indifference to the exploring of wider relationships among all forms of life. Our curiosity was no longer satisfied by the garden; we glimpsed a landscape which was not a design imposed from on high on the surface of the earth but which was the expression of many processes, natural as well as human.

How did this disenchantment first manifest itself? The familiar answer is that we discarded the formal pleasure garden in favor of the informal picturesque landscape garden, the garden as a miniature version of the natural environment, full of topographical and botanical surprises. But the picturesque landscape garden or park, however beautiful and appealing it might have been, was not the true successor to the traditional garden. Not only was it a much larger, much more expensive creation, within the reach of very few; it rejected all of the essential characteristics and functions of the garden as it had evolved through the centuries: it even eliminated the visible enclosure in order to include the entire landscape. It eliminated the garden's social role in order to cater to the solitary, individual emotional response to unspoiled nature, and it eliminated all cultural reminders, traditions which were transmitted through work and interaction, in order to produce a timeless, non-historical setting. The picturesque landscape garden which evolved in 18th Century England represented a delayed counter-attack; if in the 16th Century horticulture had triumphed over agriculture, the invasion of the park and garden by the lawn represented the triumph of the pastoral landscape, the triumph of sheep over horticulture.

No; if we want to follow the evolution of the common garden, of the archetype, we have to look elsewhere. We have to return to the primitive form of the European garden as it evolved in another part of the world. We have to study the garden in America beginning in Colonial times when it served its basic purposes — the protection of the group, the providing of food and materials, and the transition between the community and its surrounding environment.

A great deal of valuable work has been done in recent years on the Colonial gardens of Virginia and New England. What remains to be done is investigation of the gardens of the Blacks, and of the Spaniards of the Southwest — not in terms of their ornamental features but in terms of their adjustment to the American environment and to the gardens of the American Indians. In many ways the common garden in the New World evolved like the European garden: its palisade provided protection and a sense of territoriality to the first settlers, the plants and trees imported from the Old World insured the preservation of an established way of life and supplemented the scanty resources of the early farmer, and eventually the early European-American garden expanded into the surrounding world. But whereas in primitive Europe the first gardens had served to link the farmer and the herder to the village and eventually to enrich the culture, in Colonial America the garden was confronted by a strange and unpredictable forest environment, and was obliged to play the role of frontier outpost, a defense against a hostile world. It is fashionable in environmental circles to decry the heavy-handed destruction of the aboriginal ecosystem, and to accuse the early settlers of unusually vicious attitudes toward nature, and it is undoubtedly true that the transformation of the natural landscape of North America was often a warlike action, violent and without compromise. But we underestimate the bewildering problems which confronted the Colonial farmer and gardener: the unforeseen infestations of insects, the rapid increase of predatory birds and animals, the new diseases produced by even the most modest introduction of European farming methods. As E. L. Jones writes, "Prehistoric migrants had moved with their crops, animals, and whole 'living entourage' from southwest Asia into forests of northern temperate Europe. Clearing and taming that environment, for all that it is a gentle one, took a couple of thousand years. ... Repetition of fundamentally the same processes in the temperate forests of America took only two hundred years.... What European man did in America was to clear and keep clear much more of the forest than had ever been disturbed before and to bring in unfamiliar species, for example, weeds in the feed for cattle carried on shipboard.... The white settlers' fields and livestock increased feeding opportunities, and predators clustered about them in greater numbers." [6]

The exploration of the common or household garden is a way

of returning to origins, of seeing the archetypal garden once again. We have much to learn about how the common garden served to bridge the enormous geographical and cultural gap for the settlers who left 17th Century Europe behind and confronted the North American wilderness, and how it allowed them to transplant household values and household customs. The early German gardens in Pennsylvania were, many of them, belated examples of the medieval herb garden, strongly influenced by ancient astrological doctrines and ancient medicinal folklore; how much of those survive today? The Appalachian garden, a blend of imported English and native Indian ethnobotanical wisdom, still flourishes in many parts of the South, and is only now being discovered by folklorists and cultural geographers. The Mexican garden, noteworthy for its many Spanish, Indian and Mexican components, survives, almost unstudied, in remote villages of the Southwest and in the barrios of Los Angeles, Phoenix, San Antonio and other cities. Least known of all our indigenous American gardens, and in some ways the richest in variety, is the garden of the Blacks; dating back to the earliest years of slavery, it contains plants from Africa and the West Indies, and it has served to acclimatize many tropical and sub-tropical vegetables, flowers and fruits. Nor should we overlook the gardens put in by the innumerable counter-culture communities. Most of them are relatively inaccessible, and almost always short-lived, but their value lies in the number of plants they contain that are used in crafts no longer generally practiced. For many minorities — Chinese, Indian, Filipino and no doubt Vietnamese — the household garden represents the only visible link with the past that they can retain: for not only do these gardens produce plants essential to the traditional diet, they help re-establish family cooperation in work and leisure, and serve as the place — and the occasion — for the passing on of traditional nature knowledge.

Few such gardens are impressive from the point of view of design; that is a poor reason for examining them. Their economic importance is confined to a small and often needy element in the population. But they remind us of what we have all too often forgotten: that the archetypal garden is much more than a botanical display, a work of art: it is a micro-landscape, and when we recognize it as such we begin to acquire that diversity of definitions of the garden that is so necessary if we are to recognize its universal significance.

Contrasted with the farm or the park, the garden is inevitably lacking in largeness of scale and in visual appeal. In the garden the seasons succeed one another entirely without those breaks and celebrations which once punctuated the farmer's year and which are still the stuff of folklore. We must content ourselves with a place which by its nature is intimate and small and domestic. Whenever we search the garden for mythical reminders, whenever we search for traces of the Garden of Eden or the wilderness experience or of a mystical state of being, we are searching in the wrong place. The garden satisfies the aspirations of everyday existence: work shared with a few companions, family or neighbors, work that has quality and measure, capable at best of humanizing a small fragment of nature. The garden is where we can impart to others our knowledge of a family tradition, and where we can briefly withdraw from the perplexities of the outside world; it is where we plant a seed which we hope will someday flower into a more beautiful landscape, and a more harmonious community.

Gardens to Decipher and Gardens to Admire

REGARDLESS OF ITS LOCATION, the ornamental or pleasure garden — what Bacon called the princely garden — belongs to the city. It is an expression of urban values and of an urban way of life; it is a space created by urban tastes and intellect, and it flourishes whenever and wherever cities are powerful and rich.

But before the pleasure garden appeared on the scene in the 17th Century, and after the medieval garden had fallen into decay, there existed, for perhaps no more than two or three generations, a garden of a transitional style. Though it was common throughout western Europe, most histories of garden design dismiss it as without botanical or esthetic merit. Yet I think it deserves a more sympathetic treatment. It not only provides a link between two very dissimilar idioms, it illustrates how people reacted to the first discovery of the environment in the 15th and 16th Centuries and how they sought to preserve some of the values of the past.

We are familiar with the symbolic nature of the medieval garden connected either with the castle or the monastery, and its exclusive, other-worldly character. Whatever its charm and beauty, this garden had to be deciphered to be appreciated, rather than viewed. The talents of the gardener, the astrologer, the alchemist were all involved in its composition, and to enjoy the result one needed to be a member of a small society of initiates.

The medieval villager or townsman had no part in this aristocratic garden culture; each was more concerned with useful produce. Even the occasional lily or rosebush was valued less for its beauty than for its healing properties. It was only in the 13th

Century, when cities were expanding, that it can be said that a truly urban garden made its appearance.

It was, usually, a small space wedged in between houses or next to the wall of the town, where herbs and vegetables and fruit trees were grown, and chickens and geese were kept. It probably resembled what we once called a kitchen garden: a secluded area back of the house, protected by a wall or hedge.

However, it served what in those days was a novel purpose. It was a place for family recreation and sociability, and the pursuit of semi-rural hobbies. As towns grew in density the more prosperous merchants and officials bought land in the suburbs, laid out small gardens and built summerhouses. The garden villas in the outskirts of Florence that Boccaccio described were in fact very early examples of these resorts. It was in 11th Century Italy that the first guilds of professional gardeners were formed.

The emblem of a gardeners' guild was not the trowel or the spade. It was the hatchet, a tool used in the construction of arbors and trellises, both very popular in urban and suburban gardens. Although there was a growing emphasis on display, on exotic plants, ingenious hydraulic works, and topiary art, there was also emphasis on methodical cultivation of fruits and vegetables. The advent of the professional gardener in the late Middle Ages indicated that gardening demanded increased skill and taste.

By the 16th Century almost every city or large town was encircled by a zone of such gardens. Though most of them were modest in size, some were as large as twenty acres, and many were open to the holiday public which came on foot to enjoy the fresh air and to drink wine in the shade of the arbors. A late innovation was the building of one or more terraces, each set aside for a particular type of plant, and each affording a view of the surrounding countryside. Square or rectangular beds were fashionable, their edges sharply defined by borders of herbs or of brightly colored pebbles.

Well into the 17th Century almost all urban and suburban gardens had at least one trait in common — they paid less attention to flowers than to herbs and trees and vegetables. Referring to one such suburban resort, Edmund Gosse wrote that "even the famous gardens of Vauquelin des Yveteaux close to Paris were said to contain more melons than tulips, and more cabbages than hyacinths." [1]

This neglect of flowers, so foreign to our own feeling for the garden, has often been commented on. Geoffrey Grigson writes: "The pure flower-garden, the garden of absolute pleasure, the garden altogether divided from utility, is a very late fancy of the human mind. It began as a perquisite of kings and noblemen. In our own language a garden is first an enclosure, a garth, a yard (as we still say in vine*yard*) in which plants were grown — plants to eat, plants to dose oneself with, plants magically useful, even as well plants to delight by their inflorescence. It may be startling to learn that the composite word 'flower-garden' does not appear until late in the seventeenth century." [2]

How is one to account for the earlier delight in herbs, and the shift in taste which brought the cultivation of flowers into favor? It has been pointed out that herbs were essential to medieval medicine and were much used in cooking, and Grigson (as well as others) suggests that flowers, since they served no utilitarian purpose, represented an expense and a responsibility few small gardeners cared to assume. There are those who explain the attitude in ethnic or historical terms, suggesting that the love of flowers and their cultivation was originally a Mediterranean trait, appropriate to a mild climate and an agriculture based on the growing of many plants, and that it was only adopted by northern Europe after prolonged contact with Latin civilization, and even then only by the more educated classes. Heyne observes: "That the Germanic peoples had no close affiliation with the plant world of their environment, as would naturally have developed out of any gardening activity, is clearly shown in the characteristics of early Germanic art. Its ornamentation, from the so-called Bronze and Iron Ages up until the Merovingian period, consists entirely of elegant and imaginative linear motifs along with motifs adapted from human and animal forms, but never of motifs derived from plants, never a leaf, a flower, a vine or branch.... And this deficient sense of the beauty of the plant world, this contempt for that sort of growth, suggests that the Germanic peoples never grew plants except out of necessity." [3]

There was still another, simpler reason for preferring herbs to flowers: herbs are stronger smelling and have a more distinctive taste; they betray their essence to more of our senses than do flowers, whose appearance is more often a disguise than a revelation.

But all plants, according to ancient philosophy, had remarkable healing powers for mankind. Each of them grew and flowered under the influence of one of the planets which produced one of the four humors: the sanguine, the phlegmatic, the choleric, the melancholy. Furthermore, each plant was the product of one of the four elements: water, air, earth, and fire — or sunlight. Thus each of them presented a balance between cosmic and terrestrial forces. Each, however, contained a special combination, and it was essential to know the preponderance of elements and humors. Taste or smell was the most reliable guide: a plant was classified as hot or cold, dry or moist; a mouth-puckering, bitter-tasting herb would be called "cold," and a peppery, stinging herb would be called "warm," or "hot." Plants (like cress) in running water were thought to possess heat, whereas plants from the sea were "cold" because of their salt content. Most plants with a strong fragrance — caraway, fennel, dill, celery — were thought of as dry. Each plant was believed to cure diseases deriving from an imbalance in the four elements, or an excess in one of the humors. Burton's *Anatomy of Melancholy* provides a lengthy discussion of how that particular humor could be mitigated, and one cure which he described involves the use of such herbs as "borage, bugloss, balm, succory (or chicory), endive, violets, in broth, not raw." [4]

How would we know which herb to use for a particular ailment? By its external characteristics: that is to say, each plant had its sign, its signature, corresponding to its inner qualities. Indeed it was part of the philosophy of the period that every object in nature was in a sense symbolical, its appearance a signature. Paracelsus, the 16th Century physician and mystic, based much of his medical and religious doctrine on the ancient doctrine of signatures. He wrote: "It is not God's will that all He has created for the benefit of man and has given him as his own should remain hidden. And even if He did conceal some things, He left nothing unmarked, but provided all things with outward, visible marks, with special traits. . . . We men discover everything that lies hidden in the mountains by the external signs and correspondences, and thus also do we find the properties of herbs and everything that is in stones. There is nothing in the depths of the seas, nothing on the heights of the firmament, that man is unable to discover." [5]

Thus a plant with yellow flowers was good for jaundice; the liver-shaped leaves of the anemone indicated that it was good for the treatment of liver complaints, etc. The taste or odor was also a signature. "The strength which is given to bodies by means of smell," Paracelsus declared, "quickens the blood, rouses the heart, and fortifies it more than can be described." Although some botanists and physicians dismissed the more fanciful of the interpretations of signatures as superstitious, it was widely conceded throughout the 16th Century that many ailments could be cured by proper use of herbs — and that there was even the possibility of curing diseases, including the plague, by the correct compounding of perfumes. The extraordinary popularity of tobacco when it was first introduced in the last years of the 16th Century to Europe can be largely ascribed to its supposed value as a dry warm herb, especially suited to the cure of lung and head complaints. First appreciated as a scent (or as snuff) tobacco was soon identified with one of the four elements — air in the form of smoke. A 17th Century writer described its medical benefits: it "drives out all ill-vapors but itself, draws down all bad humors by the mouth, which in time might breed a scab over the whole body." [6]

These theories, especially when elaborated in a more systematic form in the 16th Century, had their effect on the landscape and on the discovery of landscape characteristics. There developed the belief that foreign or exotic herbs, imported from Asia or Africa, were simply fashionable, and less effective than those which were indigenous and of traditional use. Burton notes that the German botanist Fuchs (who gave his name to the fuchsia) wrote that "many an old wife or country woman doth often do more good than our bombast physicians with all their prodigious, sumptuous, far-fetched, rare, conjectural medicines." When Fuchs came into a village, he "considered always what herbs did grow most frequently about it, and those he distilled in a silver limbec." Burton mentions with approval the increase in the number of "public gardens ... wherein all exotic plants almost are to be seen," and studied by young students of medicine.

In keeping with this new approach to the cultivation of indigenous medicinal herbs was the greater attention given to the layout of gardens — particularly herbal gardens — a matter less of developing a pleasing spatial design than of arranging to surround the garden with rue because its bitterness would drive away all "poisonous creatures." The esthetic contribution of the herb's deep green color was secondary. Winds from the south and east were to be excluded, for they produced weakness and despondency, and though the north wind was unfavorable to fruit it was good for the health of human beings.

In many respects the 16th Century was the heyday of the cult of herbs, the age when they were most treasured in medicine, in cooking and in garden ornamentation. An English garden of late in that century is said to have contained no less than four hundred varieties of herbs. Gosse observes: "It will be found that flowers as such, without regard to their properties and medical uses, are very much neglected in the old botany books. Great value was then set on strongly perfumed plants, such as lavender, marjoram, thyme, and sage, for bordering. . . . The Elizabethans liked their flowers to have a very full scent. There seems to be evidence that they valued this even more than brilliant color. Hyacinths, which were called 'jacinths,' were looked askance at, at first, because they had little odor. . . . Their scent was doubtless the prime reason for the extreme popularity of pinks and carnations." [7]

Herbs thus provided the garden with fragrance and a familiar set of symbols; yet this was not enough to satisfy the appetite for signs and signatures. The garden itself was designed and redesigned and enlarged to accommodate the wealth of symbolism contributed by art and ingenuity. Olivier de Serres, the 16th-

Century writer on agriculture, expressed his amazement at the profusion of forms in the garden — "herbs shaped into letters, designs, ciphers, coats of arms; arranged to imitate buildings, ships, boats, and other things . . . with a marvelous industry and patience." [8]

To further enrich the symbolic scene, artificial caves and grottoes, artificial "sacred" mounds, labyrinths and statues of mythical beings adorned the more elaborate 16th Century gardens. These objects were seen and admired less as curiosities or works of art than as reminders of ancestral beliefs; the garden still retained some of its legendary quality. Paracelsus like most of his generation believed in the existence of giants and dwarves. Giants were the monstrous inhabitants of the forest, dwarves were the subterranean inhabitants of the earth. Agricola, Paracelsus' contemporary and author of a celebrated book on mining engineering, described in some detail the habits of the dwarves who lived in the mines; they were not only frequently helpful to the miners, but were active in alchemy. Statues of dwarves appeared in 16th Century gardens, and their modern counterparts are essential ornaments in the gardens of middle class Germans today.

Well into the middle of the 16th Century the esoteric aspect of the garden predominated. The medicinal herb continued to be the most important plant, and the scholar and botanist determined the content of the garden just as their concern for classifying and studying, and for discovering the virtues of plants, determined its form to a large extent. As if to protect it from contact with the wider, undisciplined landscape, the garden was usually surrounded by a wall or a hedge of trees, and it ignored the view. Even its relationship to the house or castle was minimized; few gardens were located next to the residence or complemented its spatial organization, and more often than not the garden was divided into distinct, independent rectangles, each of which contained a different composition of fruit trees, flowers, herbs, vegetables or symbolical devices. The visitor was confronted with a series of surprises, of separate divisions lacking any overall unity or even a central axis.

The richer and more fashionable gardens tended to emphasize the spectacular at the expense of the symbolical; it was as if the age had become weary of looking beneath the surface to discover reality and was increasingly prepared to be fascinated and bewildered by the forms themselves. Near Viterbo is the now neglected park of the *Sacro Bosco,* the Sacred Grove, laid out in 1560 with the intention of being unique and incredible, it still contains enormous statues of monsters, giants, fabulous creatures without discernible significance, in the midst of a landscape in which every dimension, every feature was deliberately distorted — statues, architecture, the design of the garden itself. It became less a sacred grove than a bewitched forest, impossible to decipher but capable of producing a visually disturbing experience: a world of appearances without meaning.

The 16th Century garden thus threatened to become the image of a world order that was about to turn away from the traditional search for truth. The luxuriant confusion of symbols — cosmic, heraldic, esoteric; botanical, mystical, biblical — began to defy interpretation; resemblances and correspondences began to deceive, and signatures stood for nothing. The Renaissance garden slowly vanished like the Cheshire cat, leaving only its all but indecipherable symbolism behind.

There has been some justification for our neglect of the garden of the 16th Century. It requires of us that we learn how to read and interpret its design and contents, it requires that we be initiates and believers, not mere spectators. The few examples which survive in anything like their original form, with fountains and huge shapes of clipped boxwood and intricate little beds of plants (labelled as to name and use), delight us less by their beauty than by their incomprehensibility. Each is a kind of forgotten temple, gone dormant for lack of a priesthood. Each was made for the delectation of a small group of men and women, and made to keep all others out. Isolated from its workaday environment, its impact on its surroundings was always slight, and undoubtedly slighter on other types of spatial design.

This was certainly true as well of the medieval predecessor of the 16th Century garden, but the garden which succeeded it, the 17th Century pleasure garden, represented a totally new concept: in layout, in size, in its relationship to its surroundings, above all in its emphasis on the *visual* experience, it was so revolutionary that even its ostensible purpose — the providing of a place for aristocratic pleasures — was overshadowed. It did not in itself innovate; it took from every source — botany, urbanism, architecture, engineering, agriculture, forestry, theater — and brought these disciplines together in a brilliant example of the Classical landscape which was just then emerging throughout the Western world. It offered a model of what Europe hoped to become: spacious, rational, and entirely human. It was order given visible form.

The fate which overtook the vast displays of herbs in the 17th Century garden, though of no great landscape significance, illustrates how the garden of that period responded to outside influences. The earlier importance of herbs could be explained in terms of the persistence of an ancient medico-astrophilosophical tradition. It follows that the decline in the use of herbs demands a similar weighty explanation — the decree, perhaps, of a metaphysical council. But nothing so simple occurred.

One partial explanation is provided by the development in the mid-17th Century of a new medical science, sparked by Harvey's discovery or rediscovery of the circulation of the blood. This new medicine took an approach to health that eventually rejected the doctrine of humors and signatures and astrological influences and concentrated instead on the study of anatomy and chemistry, and of the use of the microscope. Yet the medicinal herb was not so much demoted as reclassified. Scientifically analyzed in terms of its chemical properties, it continued to be prescribed and used, and indeed the most exhaustive studies of the medicinal properties of plants were written in the 17th and 18th Centuries. Prestige was on the side of the newer, more scientific forms of therapy, and loyalty to herbs tended to become a matter of class and degree of education: the peasant, the forester, the hermit, the village healer did much to keep vernacular medicine alive; if herbs were no longer generally raised in formal gardens they could still be found in the fields and woods, and contact with the New World not only enormously increased their number but reinforced the belief that health was to be had by living close to untrammeled nature.

The decline of herbs in the pleasure garden was also indirectly related to other scientific developments. The problem confronting botanists and even gardeners at this time was how to devise a new and more "natural" (which is to say, a more scientific) classification for the ever increasing number of plants being discovered. Whereas in 1532 a botanist had counted a total of 240 classifiable plants, a half century later the number had increased to 3,000. In 1623 the botanist Bauhin listed more than 6,000.[9]

The old nomenclature had been based on magical or medicinal properties, on fancied similarities, or on a Classical tradition largely confined to the study of plants in the eastern Mediterranean. The steady flow of new botanical specimens from America, Africa, and Asia, and the findings of botanists exploring Europe itself, threw the tidy system of earlier scholars into the greatest confusion. Though the Classical botanists had established a taxonomy based on the effect of a plant or its use, the 16th Century sought to define plants according to their physical characteristics, which eventually led to an analysis of their structure — a procedure encouraged by the numerous illustrated books on plants that appeared toward the end of the century. Catalogs of various botanical gardens were published in France, Italy, and Germany and widely circulated, and there was a fashion for herbariums — books of pressed plants — that supplemented for scholars the frequently inaccurate or incomplete pictures. It was as if plants were acquiring a two-dimensional visibility before being experienced as living forms.

Those who bought these books were for the most part the owners of the large and elaborate pleasure gardens becoming fashionable at the turn of the century. The often sumptuous life-size illustrations of plants kindled a desire to possess them — less for their beauty than their rarity. It was in Holland that speculation in unusual and expensive plants became a profitable business. The emphasis was on one plant, one bulb, one flower after another — first tulips, then hyacinths, then carnations. Ironically enough, the strictly economic approach to the cultivation of flowers contributed greatly to botanical knowledge:

the breeding of plants with special desirable characteristics
(color or form or size), the attempts to cross varieties, or to produce new ones in order to capture the market, did much to
foster the study of the best environment for plants; and also it
led to the planting of great beds of each fashionable flower —
and to the elimination of the older, less spectacular, if more
fragrant, flowers and herbs. It was in 1608 that there appeared
in France the first book devoted exclusively to ornamental
plants, to plants which "are worthy of note only because of the
elegance of their flowers." [10]

A flood of such books ensued, books showing not merely
ornamental plants, but designs for parterres — the elaborate,
tapestry-like flowerbeds which were coming into style. The
authors offered advice on how to arrange the flowers in showy
compositions, how to plant them according to their time of
flowering, how to rotate them and care for them. Even botanical
studies concentrated, not always willingly, on the physiology
of plants and on their appearance.

With this new almost exclusive concern for the visual appeal
of the garden and its content, the art of garden design rapidly
evolved in a new direction. It became the art of views and
perspectives, the art of broad avenues extending from castle
terrace to the remotest horizon. Garden design became the
design of the landscape as background for the theater of human
interaction.

As Foucault remarks in *The Order of Things,* "it is often said
that the establishment of botanical gardens and zoological collections expressed a new curiosity about exotic plants and
animals. In fact these had already claimed men's interest for a
long while. What had changed was the space in which it was
possible to see them and from which it was possible to describe
them. . . . The natural history room and the garden, as created
in the Classical period, replace the circular procession of the
'show' with the arrangement of things in a 'table.' What came
surreptitiously into being . . . was not the desire for knowledge,
but a new way of connecting things both to the eye and to
discourse. A new way of making history." [11]

Not everyone thinks well of the 17th Century pleasure

garden. Lovers of the picturesque — and they are numerous —
criticize the garden of the Baroque period for its artificiality, its
formality and ostentation. They criticize what they consider its
almost total subjugation of nature, its glorification of the human
presence. But few deny that it is a work of art with well formulated, consistent rules and canons. And if, as I suggested,
the 17th Century garden epitomized the spatial order of its time,
those rules are worth examining.

Artificiality is certainly one of the characteristics of 17th
Century gardens; but artificiality can mean "made by man,
rather than occurring in nature"; it need not be an invidious
word. The fundamental artificiality of the 17th Century garden
was the work not only of designers but of engineers and foresters
and what we would now call agronomists. The Italian Baroque
gardens, in many ways the inspiration for the 17th Century
gardens north of the Alps, were (because of their hillside location) notable for their terraces and for their flowing and falling
water. In order to reproduce these two features in the relatively
flat countrysides of England, northern France, the Lowlands
and Germany, the talents of the soil engineer and the hydraulic
engineer were called upon. The result was the creation, throughout the 17th Century, of many large artificial land-forms and
waterworks for gardens: the levelling of hills, the transportation
of rock and earth, the draining of marshes and the digging of
vast systems of lakes, canals, reservoirs, that counted among
the technological triumphs of the age. In addition, tens of thousands of large trees were transplanted, sometimes from distant
forests, suitable soils were moved and invisible irrigation systems
were installed. As is so often the case in the creation of ornamental landscapes, the role of the engineer and plant expert in
the construction of the Baroque garden has been ignored. What
is regrettable about this is not so much the lack of recognition as
the incomplete perception we have of what the garden signified:
not merely design, but the skillful transformation of many
aspects of the environment.

Even the artificiality of the arrangement of the plant materials — the straight rows of uniform trees, the masses of uniform
flowers, the elaborate tapestry-like design of the parterres —

represents something more than the autocratic subjection of
nature. The introduction of annual flowers into the garden compelled every garden designer, every gardener, to be aware of
the growth pattern and characteristic form of every plant, to
acquire a sensitive knowledge not only of decorative affects but
of botany. It is easy to deride the artificiality of the clipped trees
all of the same size and kind; yet each composition entailed an
educated feeling for seasonal variations, for the qualities of
shade and density and color, for requirements of soil and mois-
ture and sunlight. Few "picturesque" landscape gardens or parks
ever demanded or received such skillful and loving attention.

It is upon this artificial background that the designer produced
his work; and here again the critics' accusation of formality is
essentially valid. The 17th Century garden was designed as a
spectacle — a spectacle not of natural beauties or of a collection
of rare objects, but of spatial harmony and order. The emphasis
was therefore on symmetry and correct proportion and a pleasing relationship between the parts. In keeping with that
growing desire for the aerial view which revealed the entire
composition at a glance, the garden, in the words of a 17th Century French designer, was to be seen from above as one vast
parterre, a single unit — hence the commanding position of the
castle or palace with its terrace overlooking the succession of
parterres, fountains, canals and avenues. Hence the "noble simplicity" of the design, without distracting detail or eccentricity.

Previously the garden had sought isolation from its surroundings; the castle, though near at hand, bore no compositional
relationship to it, and the encircling landscape was excluded.
In the 17th Century entirely new relationships were established.
The castle became the dominant element in the layout and
indeed determined the garden's location, so that the terraces and
avenues served to prolong the formal interior. The garden likewise did away with the barriers separating it from the outside
world and sought, if not to invade and take possession of the
landscape, at least to dominate it by means of great avenues and
vistas, reaching, in the case of Versailles, five miles from the
palace. The vista was the factor which determined the whole
design: the basis of the bilateral symmetry, the proportions of

the various divisions as they receded from the palace, the width and orientation of the avenues. If in the course of decades many pleasure gardens expanded, they almost always grew in length, to accommodate an increasingly dominant axis.

The supremacy of the axis in innumerable Classical spaces — in the design of the city as well as in that of the garden — is a familiar characteristic, and lends itself to many interpretations. Wölfflin suggests that the vista, leading as it does from the highly structured architectural focal point into the "formless and boundless" country, represents an attempt to integrate the landscape into the garden composition.[12] Others, less sympathetic with Classical culture, see it as a symbol of militarism and regimentation; but its chief role is surely the provision of an exhilarating visual experience. "Here, expressed on the canvas of nature itself," Spengler wrote, "is the same tendency that is represented in painting by the effort toward linear perspective that the early Flemish artists felt to be the basic problem of their art and Brunellesco, Alberti, and Piero della Francesca formulated. . . . It is the *point de vue* that gives us a key to a real understanding of this remarkable mode of making nature itself speak the form-language of a human symbolism." [13]

Any spatial organization as self-conscious, as calculated as the 17th Century pleasure garden, any design so clearly motivated by the desire to satisfy a particular taste inevitably raises the question of what group it is intended for. It lost little time in banishing the more utilitarian aspects of the traditional garden — the vegetables, herbs and fruit trees — to a less conspicuous location, and by the mid-century it was prepared to devote itself exclusively to the accommodation of an aristocratic society. An element in the design or management of the pleasure garden was consequently the staging of many scheduled events. In addition to its own seasonal calendar of planting and replanting and trimming, there were the festive operations of the cascades and fountains, the fireworks and processions and plays. In England and on the continent the pleasure garden, until well into the 18th Century, was the setting for innumerable celebrations: mock tournaments, masquerades, banquets, the dramatization of myths and legends, farcical imitations of peasant life. Many of the masques composed by Ben Jonson were performed in the gardens of English noblemen. "Pan would descend from amongst the cherry trees, and Panchaia be discovered rising out of a scented bed of carnations." [14] The most formal garden contained its grotto, its temple, its imitation ruin ready to serve as a background for some dramatic performance, some ballet or *tableau vivant,* and the occasion always ended with a display of fireworks, whose brief reflection in the waters of the fountains and cascades heightened the dramatic quality of the hour.

"The courtly festivals accompanied and fostered feudal garden design beginning in the 16th century," Hennebo remarks, "for the garden was at once stage and theater, backstage and audience, ceremonial ballroom and intimate salon. *Only the garden* could satisfy all the requirements of a large court festivity." [15]

The pleasure garden as setting for social interaction, as background for playing both in the sense of diversion and of acting a part: here we glimpse what was perhaps this garden's most significant function, one for which it was deliberately planned and which it fulfilled to perfection. That is to say the 17th Century garden was essentially an artificial environment designed to give form and place and visibility to the actions of a particular group of people. The group, to be sure, was composed of members of a court or an aristocratic household, but what evolved was a new relationship between theater and actors, and eventually between the city and its inhabitants, the land and the peasants who lived on it. In the garden the concept of landscape acquired a new and complex meaning.

The cult of the picturesque landscape park or garden, beginning in England in the mid–18th Century, put an end to the pre-eminence of the Classical garden of the 17th Century; its reign was thus comparatively brief, not much more than a century. But even if the style was displaced in areas of outdoor recreation and pleasure its influence persisted almost to the present, and it is worth inquiring where that particular organization of space persisted, after it had been expelled from the garden.

It is the contention of the French urban historian, Gaston Bardet, that the inspiration for the Classical design of cities came from the pleasure garden of the 17th Century. "It is by means of garden art that the men of the Renaissance and of the Classic period became aware of a new concept of space, space opening outwards as distinguished from the inward directed space of medieval towns.... If we want to witness the birth of Renaissance urban art we have to follow the thinking of those Renaissance men eagerly seeking new forms to invent or transform. Such forms exist in two guises: those drawn on paper, and those inscribed on the earth's surface and visible at a glance: that is to say, in the form of gardens." [16]

He enlarges on the theory: the earlier garden with its emphasis on tight little compartments, independent of one another, had little effect on urban design, but when gardens were designed with emphasis on an axis and on bilateral symmetry, urban architects soon saw the similarity between the avenue in the garden and the avenue in the city, and undertook to reproduce on a much larger scale the hierarchical ordering of urban spaces.

The idea deserves attention — if only because it reminds us of the close collaboration which once existed between urban design and what we now call landscape architecture, a collaboration which two centuries of anti-urban Romanticism all but destroyed.

One could, I think, object that the urban designer is under constraints that the garden designer can usually happily ignore; most urban designers (and their royal patrons) have been compelled to work with practical results in mind: traffic, accessibility, land development, defense. The significance of the similarities between the layout of the formal garden and the layout of a Classical city derive from more than strictly esthetic considerations. As Bardet himself acknowledges, it was concern for spatial organization that inspired them both: spatial organization to serve a social order as well as to produce visual beauty. The tradition of the Classical garden with its axial composition, its emphasis on large public spaces for social intercourse, its clear-cut hierarchies, provided guidance and inspiration to one generation of urbanists after another, from the age of the absolute monarchies of 17th and 18th Century Europe to the City Beautiful Movement here in America. It is still the last desperate resort of those who hope to "modernize" the sprawling cities of the Third World.

But the spatial order of the Classical garden, its clarity, its rejection of symbolism, its unlimited capacity to dignify the human presence had even larger environmental consequences: it allowed us to define objects and people in terms of their spatial relationships, allowed us — and encouraged us — to see territoriality as an essential aspect of identity. Origin and essence, whether in plants, animals, or people, were no longer the only signatures; place, position, either in the social order or in the landscape, was what gave us visibility. The Classical garden did not produce this new classification by itself, but we can, I believe, credit it with being the first coherent manifestation of a new way of organizing the world — in terms of well-defined, carefully planned spaces: nations, provinces, landscapes, gardens, and cities, each of which conferred a new kind of identity on its inhabitants, and each of which possessed its own unique visible characteristics.

The Discovery of the Street

THE IMAGE OF THE CONTEMPORARY CITY, the sign or logo which all of us know how to interpret, is a blend of cartographic abstraction and aerial view. It is a grid pattern of streets on a plain background, a criss-cross of lines, for that is all of the city we need recognize.

To the men of the Middle Ages, the most familiar image of the city was a conventionalized cluster of towers and bastions and roofs, vertical in feeling, so tightly compacted that there was no indication of the streets and spaces within it.

The gradual supplanting of that essentially architectural image (with its flatland, upwards-directed view) by our own remote view *down* from outer space is one measure of how our perception of the city has changed. It is also a measure of how, over the centuries, the city itself has changed, by the creation of public spaces — roads, streets, avenues, squares — to give it a new form and articulation.

To us an obvious difference between a rural and an urban environment is the density of the road or street network. If we perceive the city less in terms of architecture than in terms of communication, it is because we usually experience it by moving through an elaborate system of arteries that has priority over the environment of buildings; and we are justified in perceiving the city in this manner because we sense that our economic and social system — even our notions of urban environmental systems — depend in a large measure upon the existence of streets and roads and highways as means of movement and communication and of orientation.

Yet, given a different economy, a different social order, given also an esthetic unawareness of public spaces, is the arterial system (as we know it) inevitable? A community, whatever its size and sophistication, which travels on foot, transports its wares by beasts of burden, a community whose daily movements are no more extensive than the journey to work, to church, to market, to neighbors can usually get along well with a flexible and informal network of alleys, blind alleys, flights of steps, and paths. It is charming to pass through such a labyrinth of tunnels and sunlit spaces, between blank walls and gardens and open fields, part private, part public. Well into the Middle Ages the European town knew nothing else, just as until a half century ago the Moslem towns of the Near East knew nothing else, and as many traditional American Indian communities know it still.

The emergence of the city as a system of public squares and streets harks back to a time when the medieval town began to acquire a political and territorial identity. Only in a very limited sense can the European city be seen as a continuation of the Roman city — even though it may have occupied the same site and retained not only the walls and fortification but the alignment of its principal street or thoroughfare. Spatially as well as politically and economically the European city evolved in its own unique manner.

The few small towns on the continent which survived the collapse of the Roman Empire and the repeated Barbarian invasions did so largely because their fortifications provided shelter and security for the population scattered throughout the immediate countryside and because the more powerful nobles, as well as the bishops, chose them as headquarters for their administration. The earliest urban populations were therefore likely to be composed of two very distinct elements: the rural dependents of a feudal lord living in the half-ruined city much as they might have lived in their rural villages; and a body of educated and disciplined monks, priests, scholars who comprised the court or staff of the bishop or lord. These two elements not only occupied separate areas of the town — the castle and the cathedral versus the working and farming or gardening area — but were ruled by different codes of law.

Another reason for the partial survival of some of the

Roman cities was their location: on what was left of the old roads and at established river crossings or landing places. To travelling merchants, who managed to survive the almost complete disruption of society after the 5th Century and continued to maintain contacts throughout Europe and the Near East, these riverside communities, however small and poor, offered a place to rest and to store their wares — salt, spices, weapons, honey, oil, and furs. For most of the year the merchants were far away, but their annual reappearance was often an occasion for a fair and a certain amount of trading. In time they established permanent headquarters outside the city walls near the waterfront; this merchants' village was known in northern Europe as a *vicus* — as evident in such place names as Brunswick, Norwich, Greenwich. In the 7th Century riverside London was known as Lundenwik. In western Europe the usual term for this merchants' settlement was *portus,* from which of course we derive our word for harbor. The traders, foreign or otherwise, were made welcome. Their village — actually little more than a collection of storehouses and shelters — was recognized as part of the town even if outside its walls, and in time the Crown granted the merchants their own separate legal status and their own courts. It was characteristic of the age that the Merchants' Law applied to persons only, not to the village itself; it was only in the 12th Century that it acquired a territorial character.

The advent of the *vicus,* the merchants' quarter, marked the beginning of a new development: the multiplication not so much of districts or sections in the town as of legally defined groups. The lords in the castle, the bishop and his clerical staff, had their special law; so did the feudal working population dependent on those centers of power. There was a special law for outsiders — individuals who lived and worked in the town but who were not burghers or citizens; a law for visitors, a law for Jews, and of course a law for the burghers or citizens themselves. The craftsmen and small local merchants eventually managed to free themselves from their feudal ties and to become associated with the merchants, thereby sharing *their* legal status. Even the workers and craftsmen who settled immediately outside the city walls had a status of their own.

What held each of these various groups together was mutual dependence or a common objective: territorial identification was rare. "The boundaries of these political unities, manors, feudal states, kingdoms are not yet fixed," writes Jacques Ellul. "There are therefore very few established structures. The milieu in which men live and in which institutions develop ... is based on the relationship between man and man.... It is toward the end of the 11th century that the situation changes completely." [1]

Perhaps the first evidence we have of this change — of the city evolving from a fluid assembly of legally defined groups or orders into a composition of well-defined spaces — is the appearance in the 11th Century in one northern European town after another of a recognizable, permanent marketplace. In earlier times merchants periodically offered their wares for sale in the *vicus* or in any sufficiently wide street, and local craftsmen joined them, though their production was scanty. But a combination of economic and political circumstances fostered the creation of distinct, centrally located spaces for this sort of activity. The surrounding villages, in the 11th Century, began to produce a surplus of vegetables, livestock, certain raw materials that they sought to dispose of in the nearest town; the town craftsmen likewise produced more than their feudal lords could consume, and merchants discovered that the town, now grown larger, offered a respectable outlet for their goods.

Thus the marketplace came into existence. At first little more than a widened street or open space in the *vicus,* it then moved into the town itself to be nearer its customers and sources of supply; and finally in the 11th Century, in many of the numerous new towns laid out in central Europe and France and England, we see a rectangular public place, often in the very center, where regular markets could be held. And eventually there are several markets — livestock market, grain market, crafts market, even hay market, wood market, etc.

These public spaces, undoubtedly the first planned and designed public spaces to appear in the European city, were of

course the creation of the civic authorities — a recognition not
only of the importance of the mercantile and craft interests,
but also of the fact that they demanded recognition in terms of
space. This is what the geographer Vance terms the *process of
congregation*: "The activities that grow up in limited areas of
specialization drawn into a congregation by the internalizing
linkages among them. . . . A few persons doing a particular
thing, normally congregate, but not in an obvious congregation.
When numbers are increased to the point they present a really
extensive pattern, then a geographical congregation is to be
seen." [2]

Several features of the medieval market are worth noting.
First, it was usually located in the center of the town, not
in front of the cathedral or the castle, but as often as possible —
particularly in the designed new towns of the 11th and 12th
Centuries — at the intersection of the two main streets or highways. It was located, in other words, where workaday activity
was concentrated and where many related businesses and
occupations naturally congregated: workshops, storage facilities,
inns, taverns, brothels. The market by its nature attracted
out-of-town visitors, men looking for work, pedlars, entertain-
ers, preachers, and peasants in town for the day. If in subsequent periods the marketplace became the location of public
buildings and the houses of guilds, it still remained what it
originally was: a secular space identified with the everyday
business of making a living and spending money. It is *not*
the medieval equivalent of the Classical forum, and medieval
records usually refer to it not as *forum* but as *mercatus*.

In Classical cities the forum was a space from which merchants and craftsmen were usually excluded and which was
reserved for a superior order of citizens: for political action and
the exchange of ideas. Unlike the Classical city, the European
city has always had more than one focal point: the castle or
palace or cathedral or the university corresponded to the forum;
the marketplace corresponded to those spaces in the contemporary city where transients and natives, buyers and sellers,
workers and employers, people in search of pleasure and excite-

ment all foregathered — an essential environment, which, in one shape or another, has persisted to this day.

The emergence of the marketplace in the 11th Century was significant of several developments in the medieval landscape: the importance of the merchant and craftsman in the economic life of the town was thereby recognized and given form; the self-awareness of the town or city fostered an awareness of environments, of the feasibility of planning and creating environments for special activities or groups of people. Was there perhaps also a technological significance? Did the marketplace begin to assume importance when means of transportation improved? Ever since 1924, when the French historian Lefebvre de Noëttes started to investigate the development of horse harnesses in Europe and especially the introduction of the horse collar, archeologists and historians of medieval culture have been debating the impact of those innovations. In Greece and Rome and until probably some time in the 10th Century in western Europe, men harnessed their horses to the plow or wagon by means of a collar which all but strangled the animal when the load was heavy. The new style horse collar removed the pressure from the windpipe and placed it on the shoulder blades of the horse. What ensued from this new kind of harness (which probably originated in Asia and was copied by European farmers in the Dark Ages) was the greater use of the horse as an animal of traction, in preference to the stronger but slower and less enduring ox.

In describing what he calls "The Discovery of Horsepower," Lynn White enumerates some of the very far-reaching consequences of the introduction of the new type horse harness. "We still know very little in detail about the improvement of wagons which followed the invention of modern harness, the development of pivoted front axles, adequate brakes, whipple-trees, and the like. . . . But beginning with the first half of the twelfth century we find a large, horsedrawn, four wheeled 'longa caretta' capable of hauling heavy loads, and by the middle of the thirteenth century a wagon normally had four wheels. . . . In still another way the new harness affected the life of the northern peasants. . . . [in the 13th Century] not only were peasants moving to neighboring cities while still going out each day to their fields: villages were absorbing the inhabitants of the hamlets in their vicinity. With the employment of the horse both for ploughing and for hauling, the same amount of time spent going to and from the fields would enable the peasant to travel a greater distance.... Deep in the Middle Ages this 'urbanization' of the agricultural workers laid the foundation for the change in focus of Occidental Culture from country to city which has been so conspicuous in recent centuries." [3] He notes still another consequence, of particular importance to towns: "Not only merchants but peasants were now able to get more goods to better markets."

Our generation has reason to know what the introduction of a new and more versatile vehicle can mean to a town or city. No doubt the introduction of wagon traffic in the early medieval town was gradual, but when it became possible to harness horses in tandem — one in front of the other — and when the pivoted front axle allowed wagons to negotiate sharper curves, then something began to happen to the town. The marketplace, first of all, was crowded with wagons maneuvering and parking. In certain regions where lumber was transported by wagon from the nearby forests the space needed for the maneuvering of the wagons and teams was extensive. "The great spaces have a monumental character," says a writer on the medieval towns of southern Bavaria. "The first impression on the visitor is astonishing and unforgettable. At the time of their creation this expanse was absolutely necessary, and can only be explained by the extensive freight traffic of the Middle Ages that needed a great deal of room. In front of the business establishments there had to be enough room for parking, for loading and unloading. The increase in traffic on market days had to be taken into account, and also the traffic passing through the town."

The new kind of traffic had its effect on the layout of the market, and even country roads leading into town were given attention; those living along their margins had to help in their maintenance. In town the important streets — often those inherited from the Roman Empire — were periodically repaired, and the ruts and holes made by wagons eliminated.

But the increasingly vital role played by the street in the medieval town derived less from its use by wagons than from the growth of the town itself; streets were laid out or widened and extended to regulate real estate activity and make land available in the form of lots. It seems likely that the market was the first formally designated open public space to appear in the medieval town, and that the artificially created street came later, largely as a result of the greater concentration of activity around the marketplace. Both spaces had their Classical predecessors; both were re-invented, as it were, at about the same period: the 11th Century. But the laying out of new streets involved a good deal more than traffic; it involved the orderly expansion of the town, new concepts of land ownership and taxation, and in the long run a new way of defining the town, and a new, more horizontal image.

In the 11th Century there were probably no more than a hundred communities north of the Alps that could qualify as cities, and with the exception of London and Paris and Cologne and one or two other places in the Lowlands none had more than two or three thousand inhabitants; most were little more than large villages.

Small size did not prevent them from playing their essential role as focal points in the landscape, nor from being proudly conscious that they were centers of authority and wealth, and symbols of Christian culture. Oblivious to their actual form and appearance, they saw themselves as miniature versions of a celestial prototype: a walled city divided by two intersecting streets into four quarters. A historian of the early medieval city calls our attention to the way in which the age perceived a cruciform layout even when it did not in fact exist. He cites a description of the English town of Chester, written in 1195. "It offers what is surely the most complete definition of a medieval city layout. Twice the author indicates the cross symbolism of the place: once in the city itself in the intersection of the streets that divide it into four quarters and produces four gates (just as the mystery of the Cross fulfills the double law of the Covenant in the four evangelists) and then in the

four monasteries outside the city.... The planned circle or outer
ring of churches is the hallmark of [the early medieval] town.
That it was planned and that the circle with the central castle
or 'burg' was to be perceived as a unit is attested to in eleventh
and twelfth century sources.... The loosely distributed surrounding suburban churches ... located on conspicuous topographical features transform the town and its surroundings into
a Divine landscape [*Gotteslandschaft*] whose silhouette, even
at a distance, announces the religious nature of the place ... it
was characteristic of the early medieval town that it emphasized
its vertical image."[4]

This is probably why the medieval artist in depicting such
towns showed only those buildings — castle, cathedral, churches,
fortifications — which were built of stone and which reinforced
the image of the town as a collection of towers.

But the facts of the case were very different. Towns were
not neatly divided into four quarters nor were they compact;
and permanent, stone structures were few. The castle, the
cathedral, the market, represented separate and distinct centers
of activity, and beyond them the town was little more than
small groups of flimsy dwellings, gardens and orchards; even
within the boundaries of the town or city there were totally
empty, unused stretches of land. The scale was astonishingly
small: Cambridge with a population of less than three thousand
had no less than thirteen parishes.

In the 11th Century the average dwelling in a town was very
similar to the peasant village dwelling — a small and primitive
structure of wood and clay and straw. These buildings were
usually huddled together in compounds, grouped in close-
packed neighborhoods, according to family ties, ethnic background, or feudal allegiance. These temporary shelters were so
little thought of and accorded so little dignity that the punishment for many civil offences was the destruction of the
offender's dwelling. In times of war the houses of the poor
were often torn down as a defense measure, for fear that the
attackers would set fire to them and destroy the whole town.
Each such compound or precinct stood apart, so that the early
town resembled a collection of tight neighborhoods, not unlike

the Oriental town divided according to clans or tribes and
only partially penetrated by blind alleys and passages. What
streets existed in this mosaic of communities were narrow and
crooked and led to the center of town or the place of work,
not to neighboring precincts. The two intersecting streets or
roads leading to the outside world had an entirely different
character.

The 11th Century saw the emergence of a new kind of urban
plan, based not simply on the dominance of a small number
of important buildings and streets but on the street as a direct
link between the private domain — home or place of work —
and the life of the town. There is some debate as to how this developed, and where. Evidence indicates that, in northern France
during the first decades of the century, when a town was
expanding the landowners determined the location of streets
in order to produce an orderly and profitable subdivision into
lots — a practice followed in England after the Conquest.
On the other hand designed streets became common in central
Europe at about the same time, when merchants were granted
land for building houses near the marketplace. Streets devoted to one particular craft or trade became common. In any
case the discovery of the street as a determinant of city growth
and development had by the end of the century produced
increasingly orthogonal town patterns, based on right angles and
perpendicular lines — most conspicuous in the bastides or
artificial, fortified medieval towns of southern France and in
the so-called colonial towns of central and eastern Germany.

We, who live in towns and cities where the system of streets
not only provides an armature for the whole built environment but affects much of our view of the world, cannot easily
recognize the extent of that medieval revolution. Its most
fundamental result was the destruction of the former arrange-
mant of self-contained neighborhoods and precincts and the
integration of every dwelling, every resident into the life of the
town or city. The house or workshop now had direct and
permanent contact and communication with the public and was
related to a public space. It created a new kind of community.

Almost at once the town authorities recognized the street

as a versatile tool for exerting control. In one town after another ordinances regulated the height of buildings, the pitch of their roofs, their construction, even their design, which had to be suited to the social standing of the occupants. City building plans were detailed. When a highly placed citizen of Lucerne wanted to build "a simple and inexpensive house" on his own land he was informed that according to the town plan a "handsome residence" had to be built. In the additions to existing towns and in most of the new towns the dimensions of the lot were prescribed, and all houses were taxed on the basis of their frontage. The fact that each house owned half the width of the street in front of it encouraged each business or each household to expand its activities into the street and to use the space for its convenience. As a consequence the civic authorities legislated questions of health and safety.

Finally what the street did to the medieval town was introduce a more precise system of linear measurements in the sale or purchase or assessment of land, so that land came to be seen as a commodity.

The esthetic consequences of the building of streets were scarcely less revolutionary. People learned to perceive a new kind of public space where previously they had merely seen a succession of alleys and passageways, a crooked interval between houses. Now they discovered a continuous space with a quality — and eventually with a name — of its own. What had been two rows of heterogeneous structures now became the walls of a spatial unit. From the beginning therefore the street served to catalyze the confusion of houses and spaces of the early medieval town, introducing concepts of architectural orientation and harmony, and even façade. At the same time the street undoubtedly destroyed one visible bond between town and village. Speaking of the development of the European city, Spengler mentions, "the courses of the streets, straight or crooked, broad or narrow; the houses low or tall, bright or dark, that in all Western cities turn their façades, *their faces,* and in all Eastern cities turn their backs, blank wall and railing, toward the street. . . . And these stone visages that have incorporated in their light world the humanness of the citizen

himself and, like him, are all eye and intellect — how distinct
the language of form that they talk, how different from the
rustic drawl of the landscape!" [5]

It was in this tentative and almost unconscious manner that
the street in our European-American landscape began a career
that became increasingly spectacular and then culminated
in the freeway. Imperceptibly and over many generations our
vision of the city shifted from the cluster of towers and
spires to the perspective of avenues and streets and uniform-
size lots. The celestial model, never easy to discern in the dark
medieval spaces among stone walls and crowded huts, has
been at last forgotten; the map, the diagram, the coordinates are
what help us make sense of the city.

Landscape as Theater

WHEN WE SPEAK OF THE "scenes of our child-
hood," or borrow Pope's phrase and refer to the world as "this
scene of man," we are using the word *scene* in what seems
a literal sense: as meaning location, the place where something
happens. It rarely occurs to us that we have in fact borrowed
a word from the theater to use as a metaphor. Yet originally
scene meant stage, as it still does in French, and when it
first became common in everyday speech it still suggested its
origin: the world (we were implying) was a theater, and we
were at once actors and audience.

The notion that a bond exists between people and the world
they inhabit is fundamental to our understanding of life, and
the bond has usually been seen as that between parents and
children. The metaphor drawn from the theater seems to have
become popular at a comparatively late date, no earlier than the
16th Century. Its formulation implies three things: the development of the theatrical production as a formal art with its
own rules and conventions and its own environment; a widespread belief that the relationship between people and their
surroundings could be so expertly controlled and designed as
to make the comparison appropriate; and, most important of all,
the metaphor implies people's ability to see themselves as
occupying the center of the stage.

It was logical that the theater arts as we know them should
have evolved first in Italy in the early 16th Century, for it was
there that the art (or science) of perspective arose — the art,
that is to say, of defining or depicting a body in terms of
the space it occupies. The first stage sets were the work of
Italian artists and architects and technicians, and it was in Italy

that we find the first stage, the first area defined in terms of the relation between actors and audience, and in fact the first building designed exclusively for theatrical productions. For more than a century the standard theater was known as the Italian style theater; the term meant not only the building itself, but stage, scenery, the whole illusion of space achieved by the skillful use of light and color and form: the space of a make-believe world which revolved around the presence of actors.

It was surely no accident that at much the same period artists began to paint pictures of landscapes. It was Albrecht Dürer who in the course of his return from Italy first sketched from life some of the villages he travelled through. The painters of northern Europe differed from those of Italy in their interest in the everyday aspect of the landscape; they often chose as their subject village celebrations or glimpses of peasants at work in the fields, whereas the Italian painters preferred to use the rustic landscape as a somewhat remote background for more formal subjects inspired by myth or philosophy. But in both cases landscape was an element in the composition, serving to locate or define the human action. The artist modified or even restructured the background scenery in order to produce a harmony between the world of man and the world of nature.

The last decades of the 16th Century and the first decades of the 17th witnessed the development of still another form of landscape depiction: the rise of descriptive geography. Geography had previously been little more than a branch of cosmography — the study of the earth as a heavenly body. The growing interest in Classical literature encouraged the investigation and description of places mentioned in Greek and Latin texts, and a renewed study of Classical writers on geography. What first evolved was therefore a kind of historical geography. But the impact of the reports of explorers of the New World and of Asia soon expanded the field. Travelers, merchants, missionaries all contributed to a wider and more accurate knowledge of the earth's surface and at the same time supplemented or corrected Classical accounts. An abundant literature of topographical description, enriched by maps and illustrations

of cities and landscapes and exotic costumes, was the outcome
of this first wave of geographical inquiry.

It was characteristic of those early productions that they
emphasized the human or political aspects of the world: boundaries, territorial divisions, language, towns and cities. Only
insofar as they served as frontiers were rivers and mountains
mentioned. All of them dwelt on history, military or dynastic;
but history as then conceived included legends and myths. The
writings of Mandeville and Münster and of many of the early
travelers in the New World contained not only much valuable
information about little-known regions but also a large element
of the fabulous, and generalizations based on hearsay. In
the minds of the writers the distinction between fact and fancy
was neither clear nor important. Scientific accuracy was not
the aim of the descriptive geographers: they sought to make the
world visible and to inspire wonder.

From the point of view of the student of landscapes and
their evolution, the 16th and 17th Centuries represent one of
the most important periods in our Western history. It was then
that men first undertook to impose order and design on their
surroundings not merely for survival but to produce a kind of
beauty glorifying and making visible a particular relationship
between men, and between men and nature. There was scarcely
a discipline which did not contribute to the undertaking.
The artist was the first to see and depict men and women,
not as isolated figures but as dominating their environment.
It was the cartographer who delineated territories, revealing
their form and relating them one to another. It was the geographer who undertook to describe the world and the bond
between people and the land they occupied. Always the emphasis was on the visual; the world and everything in it was a
source of delight, and all that could be seen and understood
by vision was worthy of study.

In those times a word much used in the titles of books of
travel and description was *theater*. A popular textbook was
called the *Theater of Geography*, a book of pictures was called
the *Theater of Cities*. There were books called the *Theater
of Agriculture*, the *Theater of the Garden*, the *Theater of the*

World. The word of course emphasized the visual, the spectacular aspect of the environment, but it also suggested a spectacle in the sense of a dramatic production with a well-defined space, an organization of place and time, and coherent action.

Theater was thus a useful and appropriate metaphor, but more than that, it gave the ultimate three dimensional form to all the chorographic, esthetic and philosophical theories redefining men and the world. In retrospect it is clear why the drama should have been the dominant art form of an age concerned with place and visibility and the Classical image of humanity. It is clear why the theater developed new techniques of staging precisely when artists and cartographers and geographers were beginning to describe the surface of the earth. Lope de Vega wrote the *Great Theater of the World;* Shakespeare, among others, reminded us that all the world was a stage. It was in theatrical terms, therefore, that man's place could be interpreted as a work of art, his identity best established.

It is tempting to assume that this recognition of the environment and its role in establishing human identity signified a scientific interest in nature. But this does not seem to have been the case. Beautiful though the world of nature might be, it was nevertheless seen essentially as background, the realm of myth and magic. The scenery which artists, architects, engineers created on the 16th Century stage was far from realistic. It consisted of the illusion of great distances, vertical as well as horizontal, of architecture on a monumental scale, of supernatural light and movement. Even the plays of Shakespeare, though modestly produced as compared to Italian and French plays, were performed in an atmosphere of magic. Many unholy sound effects accompanied the action: bells, cannon, thunder, birdsong. The wind blew, the sea crashed, echoes resounded. Music was closely coordinated with the development of the drama and underscored the lyrical or passionate episodes. On the continent, stage designers produced impressive cloud effects with thunder and lightning and the illusion of mountains and stormy seas suddenly appearing or vanishing, or parting to reveal an elaborately costumed ballet. Pagan divinities descended from the sky, cities were consumed by fire, destroyed by earthquakes. In a Spanish production of the 16th Century, God Himself was shown, surrounded by saints and hovering angels. In a play given in Rome and staged by the architect Bernini, the entire stage was suddenly flooded.

The purpose of these elaborate illusions was to amaze and delight a public eager for visual pleasures, for the sensation of space, and to entertain those who were perhaps not able to follow the drama itself. In the early days of the new theater many conventions, carried over from court or church ceremonies, effectively destroyed any feeling of realism. Writing and acting were still inexpert. The left side of the stage was considered the most prestigious location and actors sought to stand there, regardless of the action of the play. When not reciting their lines, they frequently greeted friends in the audience, and, in fact, favored members of the audience came and sat on the stage, commenting loudly on the performance and interfering with the movements of the actors.

Nevertheless the many illusionary devices made visible to the public a world of myth and magic and history and legend; a kind of supernature more dreamt about than experienced, giving intensity and color to the action, and locating it in an imaginary realm. A superreality, an allegorical verisimilitude was the stage designer's objective, as it was that of the geographical descriptions; by associating man and his actions with an exotic or splendid setting, his importance and uniqueness were magnified. There was no attempt to explain man in terms of environmental influences, though astrological influences were generally acknowledged.

It was characteristic of the period that it defined the word landscape in another manner: *landscape* indicated both the *background* of a picture, and a stage set — that element in a composition which gave it form and suggested location but which was not of the main body of the argument.

It was while this reverent and uncritical acceptance of the world prevailed that men expressed most eloquently their delight in God's creation; in painting, in writing, in the design of gardens and in the artificial world of the theater. The

familiar landscape was thought to be no less worthy of study
and admiration than the remote and new, and provincial culture flourished as vigorously as the metropolitan. It was in
consequence a time when geographical descriptive writing enjoyed much the same sort of popularity as did the theater. A
17th Century French book on the art of conversation ridiculed
the amateur geographer who, when he had bought a beaver
hat, regaled his dinner companions with a discourse on Canada,
the fur trapping industry, discussed North and South America,
naming their principal rivers and gold mines, adding details
about their unusual flora and fauna. Atlases, and albums of city
panoramas were widely sold; fashionable ladies read books
about Persia and Siam in order to shine in society. The same
writer cautioned women against appearing *too* geography-
minded. "I permit them to use such words as *climate, zone,* and
isthmus," he wrote, "and a few others, but I do not want them
to terrify me by mentioning *longitudes* and *latitudes."*

Toward the middle of the 17th Century the metaphor of landscape as theater quite abruptly and quite radically began to
change its significance. Theater ceased to mean exclusively
spectacle and came to mean drama, the analysis and solution of
a problem. Landscape painting acquired, at least in its choice
of subjects, a formal, almost abstract quality; the plan, the detailed map replaced the panorama of the countryside and city,
as if color to charm the eye had been drained from the view of
the world. Increasingly it was presented in the black and
white of the printed word or the steel engraving.

It was in fact in the mid-17th Century that geographers
appear to have abandoned their exclusive interest in description based on observation and personal experience and to have
turned their attention to what we would now call the earth
sciences. There were practical as well as philosophical reasons
for the shift. The greatest demand for geographical expertise
came from merchants and traders engaged in foreign com-
merce, eager for more precise knowledge of tides and weather
and currents and the location of safe harbors. Both in France
and England the crown demanded geographical investigation of

strategic and political problems. The emphasis accordingly moved to research, to measurement and theory, and there was a corresponding decrease in provincial or historical writing, with its moral and religious ingredient. On the continent the influence of Descartes on geology and meteorology encouraged the rejection of the Classical heritage, as well as a skeptical approach to local sources of information. Vision itself demanded a new, scientific perspective: that of the microscope and telescope.

This turning inward, away from the world as a spectacle revealing the divine order, was also characteristic of the late 17th Century theater. Instead of seeking to establish man's central place by means of spatial illusion, the theater now resorted to intellectual means, formulating with increasing precision the doctrine of the three unities: unity of time, of place, and of action, and rejecting the magic aspects of the theater, at least in the presentation of serious drama. Tragedy demanded a small, all but empty stage with a highly formalized background — a room in a palace, a public space in the city. "As philosophers have divided the universe ... into three regions," Hobbes wrote, "celestial, aerial and terrestrial, so the poets ... have lodged themselves in the three regions of mankind, court, city, country.... From hence proceeded three sorts of poesy, heroic, schematic, and pastoral." In the heroic or tragic production interaction between the stage and the surrounding imaginary world was reduced to a minimum, as if the century were declaring that man was most clearly himself, was best identified, when the influences of the legendary environments of history and supernature were eliminated. Drama was interaction with other persons, a psychological confrontation. "The tragic palace," a historian of the 17th Century theater has remarked, "the simple decorated antechamber with four doors ... make all action and drama converge on a single point. These correspond to the severity of a plot or story line where fate has confined the protagonists to one place and condemned them to struggle against each other until death — or flight — has liberated them." The bare stage epitomizes the new abstract definition of space.

Thus with the development of a more intellectual, scientific geography, and a more intellectual, psychological type of drama the metaphor of landscape as theater ceased to be useful or appropriate. There remains, however, as a kind of epilog, the story of its final eclipse.

The popular, as distinguished from the serious or classical, theater in the 17th Century, continued to rejoice in the spectacular. An increasingly exaggerated celebration of the mythical historical landscape, particularly in opera and ballet, eventually led to even more grandiose productions, with the result that on the popular level the staging, the scenery — the landscape in the theater sense of the word — threatened to overwhelm the actors and their not very significant dilemmas. The fascination with illusion inevitably led to a fascination with deception. Plays of little quality went to infinite pains to achieve meticulous realism in staging: scenery, props, and costumes reproduced in pedantic detail regional or historical settings — China, the New World, ancient Greece, scenes from the Bible. Accents and gestures sought to reinforce the illusion, and actors, like figures in a historical pageant were reduced to little more than props. A century earlier the scenic environment, whether on the stage or in the landscape, had served to highlight and intensify the identity of the protagonists: now, identity was seen as a matter of conformity to a given environment, a blending into it.

We can, in fact, indicate with some precision the moment when this reversal was complete. In 1799, Robert Fulton, the American inventor, brought the first large diorama to Paris. A grandiose, circular panorama of New World scenery, accurate in every detail and without the disturbing presence of a single actor, it was an immediate success. Within a short time a theater was opened devoted exclusively to dioramas, one of its rules being that no more than two actors were ever to be allowed to appear in front of the scenery. The theater was dedicated "to the reproduction on a theatrical scale of those views which are most worthy of exciting public curiosity from the historical and picturesque point of view."

Significantly enough, one of the men who helped organize

the theater was Daguerre, soon to make a name for himself as a pioneer photographer.

This first theater without actors, devoted to the display of landscapes without people, marks the appearance of a totally new definition of landscape: natural scenery which man should not contaminate by his presence. It also marks the appearance of a new kind of drama — one which takes place in a domestic interior and involves domestic and psychological problems, hidden from the public world. And with the final rejection of the Classical metaphor of landscape as theater the search was on for a new and more vivid way of defining the landscape.

We are still searching. All that we have so far come up with is an analog of one sort or another, borrowed from biology or ecology or communication theory. When it is a matter of controlling or manipulating the environment, analogs can be extremely helpful; yet if we are again to learn how to respond emotionally and esthetically and morally to the landscape we must find a metaphor — or several metaphors — drawn from our human experience. The fact that we have so far failed to do so is no cause for despair. As history should teach us, and particularly the history of art, it is largely a matter of chronological perspective. It was only in the 19th Century that men perceived the rightness of the theater metaphor as applied to the 16th and 17th Century concept of landscape. It is only now that we are acquiring sufficient perspective on the 19th Century to understand that landscape in terms of a metaphor of growth and decay and evolution. It is still too early to understand the new 20th Century landscape. We can best rely on the insights of the geographer and the artist and the philosopher. They are the most trustworthy custodians of the human tradition; for they seek to discover order within randomness, beauty within chaos, and the enduring aspirations of mankind behind blunders and failures.

The Sacred Grove in America

As we all know, there are scores of places in the United States whose names include the word *grove*. There is Pacific Grove, California; Council Grove, Kansas; Webster Grove, Missouri; and Asbury Grove, Massachusetts. There are many places with such names as Grove City and Groveton and Grove Center, and there are Groves of every kind of tree: Cedar, Maple, Willow, Pine, Walnut, and so on.

A few are sizable towns; most of them are small, little more than crossroads hamlets. The majority of them, I think, are to be found in the deep South, and in Arkansas and Texas and Oklahoma. Even there they are well hidden. Travelling through the piney woods we often see a hand-painted sign pointing to Pleasant Grove or Shady Grove. If we follow the narrow dirt road we find the grove to be simply another part of the forest. Perhaps there is an overgrown clearing nearby.

For years I wondered about the profusion of groves. Many of us look to Europe for origins and influences when we are confronted with something rural, and especially to English origins. But aside from a romantic tradition of druidical groves and Milton's "Olive Grove of Academe, Plato's retirement," English has little to offer.

I eventually discovered that the existence of groves in 19th Century America had nothing to do with fashion or literary allusion. The grove was usually the site of a revival or a camp meeting, and possibly of a church as well. Revivals and camp meetings were, and still are, important events in much of rural America, attracting hundreds, even thousands, of people, and often lasting several days. We associate such meetings with the first decades of the 19th Century when they proliferated all over frontier America, but they are of common occurrence even now. The deserted clearings in the woods often come to life in the fall of the year. So the place name is actually much more than a mere place name. It indicates a particular *kind* of place, and to many people it serves as a reminder of an important event in their lives: a profound and often decisive religious experience.

What that experience is or was I am not qualified to discuss. What interested me in this matter, and long perplexed me, was the choice of location: a wooded outdoor setting of no outstanding scenic quality. It is true that many religious gatherings have taken place outdoors, have taken place, in fact, in groves. But the practice seems to have been more pagan than Christian. Classical antiquity made much of sacred groves. Fraser took one of them, not far from Rome, as the inspiration for the *Golden Bough,* and Martin Nilsson in his book on Greek piety tells us that sacred groves were scattered throughout the Greek landscape. "Many places of worship," he says, "had not even a modest chapel. The image of the god, if there was one, stood under the open sky.... Trees growing in the sacred precinct were protected and could not be cut down; so a grove, in a landscape so ill-supplied with timber as Greece, was often synonymous with a holy place." [1] There was certainly no lack of trees in Appalachia, and the first thing done, once the spot for a camp meeting had been chosen, was to cut down many of the trees and convert the stumps into benches for the congregation. Perhaps the origin of the American grove lies deeper in our European heritage than we had thought. In both cases, in Greece as in Kentucky, the grove had a religious character.

But then Nilsson says something disconcerting: "We make a spot holy by putting a sanctuary there; but in Antiquity the holiness belonged to the place itself, and a sanctuary was erected there *because* the spot was holy. Zeus was surnamed *after* the mountains about whose summits he gathered his clouds."

Thus, the reason for considering a grove sacred in America was almost the direct opposite of the reason the Greeks had for considering *their* grove sacred. *Place* in antiquity came first; the deity and his or her shrine came later. In Christendom it was *action,* human or divine, that sanctified a place. With us, in the beginning was the word — or the deed.

The widespread traditional belief that certain spaces are inherently sacred is examined in detail by Mircea Eliade.[2] It is a belief which affects very strongly the organization of the human landscape. A sacred space, whether grove or mountain or spring, becomes the focus of settlement and thus produces a community and a ritual based on territoriality — a space occupied by a well-defined group. It establishes a hierarchy among the surrounding spaces. The nearer a space is to the sacred spot the more desirable it becomes. Space thus tends to develop a centripetal pattern; in the design of the cosmos and in that of the landscape and of the sacred precinct itself. And it follows, I think, that this kind of spatial organization helps determine the social organization, which becomes hierarchical and centered upon the symbol of authority. Progress toward the sacred, or toward power, whether we understand progress in terms of motion or of development, assumes the form of passing through spaces or grades of increasing sanctity until the center is reached.

Finally, time itself is organized to remind us of the sanctity of space: the day, the year, the lifespan are measured in terms of the recurring passage of time from one pre-ordained space to another. The calendar marks the location of heavenly bodies at certain seasons and determines a succession of rites and ceremonies, definite stages or positions in the existence of the individual as well as in that of the community. The phrase "to be in Seventh Heaven" must once have had such a significance: the point where spatial and temporal goals coincide to produce something like complete bliss. Yet here again the emphasis is more on the moment.

This way of perceiving the design of the world implies that religion is a public, almost a political, matter. No doubt at the beginning the ceremony was a family gathering based on a feeling of a common territory. But later it became the concern of the state or its equivalent. Religion thus acquired a civic character, and its rites became a blending of processions through public spaces and of public observances of cosmic feast days, all of them confirming the sanctity and relationship of ordered space and ordered time. Furthermore, all communication with the deities had to occur in a recognized public sacred place. Moses forbade all private sacrifices. "Take heed to thyself that thou offer not thy burnt offering in every place that thou seest, but in the place which the Lord shall choose in one of thy tribes." And Plato, in *The Laws,* was even more explicit: "No one is to possess a shrine of his own in his own home. When a man takes it into his head to offer sacrifice he is to go to the public shrine to do so." I suspect the rule had two objectives: to preserve the spatial uniqueness of the shrine, and to preserve the timetable against the distortion of the calendar by private, unscheduled rites.

In a well-ordered traditional society therefore not much importance is attached to the private religious experience, but neither is there much concern over heretical beliefs. Any divinity could be worshipped, provided the service was done in a sanctified space; anything could be celebrated, provided the celebration occurred at a sanctified time.

This concept of the cosmos as a harmonious ordering of sacred space and time has been often described; the point I wish to make is that the emphasis in certain societies is on the priority of *space.* These are what we now call conservative societies, determined to maintain an order which they conceive of as divine and based on place and position in space. The overriding question in such a religion as well as in everyday life is status; the question to which everyone seeks an answer is *Where?*

It is when the question assumes a different form, when we start searching for the answer to *When?* that the picture changes. Time and the ordering of time then become more important than the ordering of space. Why this change occurs, why the private, personal concern with the *When* becomes more actual than the traditional public concern with the *Where* is a problem which historians can no doubt explain. But it frequently occurs: and one of its first signs is a decentralization of space. The organization of space becomes a strictly social matter, a way of maintaining an order which is social rather than divine.

Colonial America, particularly Colonial New England, offers a very good example of this transition — part religious, part political — between two attitudes. The notion of *sacred* space was already on its way out when the first settlers arrived in the New World, but space in political or social terms was still highly conservative and almost Classical. The manner in which the church edifice was defined suggests the shift. It was impossible, even when faithfully reproducing the Classical concentric space of the village or town, to identify the church building with the temple or shrine. Christian doctrine, being based on the omnipresence of God, implied that *all* spaces were sacred, just as all time was sacred. Both had a historical beginning and were progressing toward a historical end. The church was therefore defined not as a building, but as the function, the content: defined as the congregation. Cotton Mather found "no just ground in Scripture to apply such a trope as church to a house for public assembly." [3] Others agreed with him, and meeting house was the term generally adopted. Most of us have backslidden in this usage, but the distinction is still emphasized in some evangelical sects. The inscription "The Church of Christ Meets Here" is common throughout America — as if to remind us that no place is in itself especially sacred; only its use is sacred.

But the political role of the meeting house substituted very well for the sacred role. It was not only the site of political gatherings; its doors and walls were adorned with legal notices, notices of sales, and announcements of public events. The seating of the congregation indicated the social status of the various families, and an elaborate and time-consuming undertaking was the annual dignifying of the church: the defining of certain seats in terms of prestige — declaring that the first row in the gallery was socially the equivalent of the first four pews on the right, and so on. The graveyard underwent the same scrutiny and so, for that matter, did any procession, funeral or academic, social or political. Even though it had no religious justification, the ordering of space in Classical hierarchical terms seems to have been of great concern to the 17th Century.

As for the ordering of time, that too was explicit, and like the sacred order of antiquity placed much importance on progress by means of gradual, publicly recognized steps to the ultimate state of redemption: baptism, instruction, periodic discipline, conversion, and communion. The Lord's Day and the evening of the Sabbath, as well as the inflexible hour of the service itself, were sacred moments. The service followed a prescribed order, and the procession within the church persisted until late into the 18th Century. Private religious services were an impossibility, since the presence of the congregation was essential.

This concern for hierarchical space and liturgical time may well have seemed to many New Englanders merely a vestige of an obsolete point of view. The real concern among certain members of every congregation might have been with that inscrutable question of *When?* The event which we know as the Great Awakening, and which lasted throughout the 1730s and 1740s in most of the Colonies, can be seen as an attempt to make *time* the essential element in the religious experience.

Theologically speaking, the Great Awakening was a complicated occurrence. For the layman the movement remains mysterious: the sudden eruption in orthodox congregations of a new kind of piety — a piety which Gaustad describes as placing "its first priority upon the direct, immediate, private and incontrovertible experience of God.... Not ecclesiastical bureaucracies but private epiphanies." [4]

Much of the movement can however be understood as a conflict between two different attitudes toward time and space: between the conservative attitude of the orthodox, who thought of gradual, pre-ordained public progress toward sanctity and attached great importance to the ordering of political space, and (on the other hand) the attitude of the dissenters, who sought a private, sudden sanctity and who were indifferent to structured space.

What was doubtless one of the most disturbing features of the new piety was its insistence on abrupt conversion — its belief that conversion, which to the orthodox meant a radical change of identity and status, could be hastened. In the words of a critic, writing in 1740, it meant "an absolute, immediate, instantaneous work — darted in upon us like a flash of lightning ... changing the whole man into a new creature in the twinkling of an eye." [5] Another minister noted that the new movement assumed "that this work of conversion or the New Birth is sudden and instantaneous and wrought by an irresistible Degree of God's Grace and Power.... For they say, that as the work of Creation was wrought in an instant ... so our second creation, likewise, must be an instantaneous work." [6] But he reminded his audience of the orthodox point of view. "Conversion," he said, "is a *progressive* work, and the principles and habits of Grace and Goodness are not infused in us by miracle, all at once.... The several Graces of Christianity are acquired by degrees, one virtue is added to another and we grow up to the Christian life by insensible gradations."

Still another assault on the established ordering of time, less significant perhaps, but no less irritating, was the irregularity and unpredictability of the services. Instead of taking place punctually at nine o'clock on the Sabbath, during the excitement of the Great Awakening they often occurred every day of the week, frequently in the evening, and the established order of the service itself was disrupted, either by the longwindedness of the preachers or the enthusiastic and unrestrained behavior of the congregation. It became impossible to establish the time of conversion and coordinate it with the necessary preliminaries.

But whereas the new concept of time produced very decided changes based on an explicit doctrine, the changes in space were by and large the product of indifference to and neglect of the traditional order. One of the most objectionable features of the movement, at least to the orthodox, was the crumbling of the notion of territoriality — the idea (again inherited from a remote past) that the church or congregation was identified with a distinct, legally defined space, the autonomous parish with its own boundaries. The first harbingers of spatial anarchy were the itinerant preachers who appeared, invited or uninvited, from outside the parish to conduct the new style of service. The Harvard faculty was incensed by this misconduct, and in Philadelphia a journalist sharply denounced the practice. The new spirit, he declared, "acts the busybody, is here and there and everywhere and above all things hates rules and good order, or *bounds and limits.*" [7]

No doubt he was thinking of the mass meetings which had occurred in Philadelphia a few years before when Whitefield had preached to a crowd which Benjamin Franklin (who was present) estimated at close to twenty thousand. In any case, the overflowing of the traditional space of the church into the surrounding outdoors, whether deliberate or not, soon became a feature of the revival services. It is hard to discover whether the outdoor setting had any effect on either the preachers or the public. From what we read, there was no trace of Romantic nature worship in the practice, no awareness that "the Groves were God's first temples." [8] All that can be surmised, I think, is that the use of outdoor unstructured space indicated a rejection of a traditional space, identified no doubt in the minds of many of the younger and poorer auditors with a social order in which they occupied the lowest and least desirable locations.

If there is anything to be gleaned from the accounts of the Great Awakening about a new relation to the environment, it comes from a study of the spatial metaphors used in the sermons. The metaphors of orthodoxy had chiefly been drawn from the Bible, but also from the military, hierarchical aspects of the social order: the embattled soldiers of God, the armies of the saints, the war against Satan. But with the Awakening strange new metaphors came into use. "What can our modern teachers mean," one conservative clergyman complained, "when they talk of *impulses,* notions and impressions, likened to pulsations of an artery, to hot water, or the motions of a foetus in the womb?" [9] As if in keeping with the outdoor surroundings and the gloom of the poorly illuminated churches in the evening, the talk was full of flashes of lightning, sudden darkness, sudden light, flashing darkness, flaming swords, blindness, and blindness all at once relieved. The arrival at a sacred place, a *destination,* was no longer the obvious sign of grace; the new symbol was the sudden presence of an overwhelming light.

It is not necessary to discuss the strange behavior of many

of the converts, the manner in which many services were interrupted by tears and outcries. These phenomena have often been associated with religious ecstacy, and in a modified form they cannot be dismissed as total aberrations. A common explanation has been that disturbances of the inner ear, as a result of violent emotion or unusual movement, can and do produce a temporary uncertainty as to orientation and relation to the surrounding environment. When it is a question of sudden change of spiritual identity, this sort of experience will be sought after and indeed artificially induced.

By 1750 the Great Awakening had begun to flag. It was not until a half-century later that the New Piety was again manifested in American life — and not so much in New England and the East as in Appalachia and the new country beyond the mountains. Historians distinguish this second episode — generally called the Great Revival — from the first, and identify it with a different population and different doctrines. Historically and theologically they are correct, but from the point of view of a concern with the emergence of a new concept of religious time and space in America and the destruction of the *old* concepts, the Great Revival was essentially a continuation and completion of the Great Awakening. No matter whether the revivals and camp meetings took place in South Carolina or Tennessee or New York, no matter whether they were Baptist or Methodist or interdenominational, they usually displayed the same attitudes toward space and time as the earlier version — though in a more vivid and more self-confident form. The site of the gathering was chosen for convenience and accessibility; many meetings took place on private land, others in barns or half-completed churches. In the sense that Mircea Eliade uses the word, the space chosen for the meeting is entirely *undifferentiated* — neither sacred nor profane — and a matter of little significance. Within the meeting itself a totally new seating arrangement was introduced. The "anxious seat," occupied by those who seriously hoped for conversion, was the place of honor and was of course temporary. As for the wider environment, the region, largely free of political boundaries, was seen as the logical field for missionary work. The itinerant preacher

and the circuit rider, travelling hundreds of miles a year, became familiar figures.

The traditional sequence of the service was eliminated: several preachers, often of different denominations, held forth
simultaneously to the immense crowd, even while singing was
underway. A most significant aspect of the growing obsession
with time was the concern with the approaching millenium or
end of the world — the end of all historical time.

Fear of damnation and hell played its usual important role,
and so did the fascination with light, now augmented by awareness of fire. A description of the famous revival at Cane Ridge,
Kentucky, in 1801 suggests something of the unreal atmosphere
prevailing: "At night, the whole scene was awefully sublime.
The range of tents, the fires, reflecting light amid the branches
of the towering trees; the candles and lamps illuminating the
encampment, hundreds moving to and fro, with lights or
torches, like Gideon's army; the preaching, praying, singing and
shouting, all heard at once, rushing from different parts of the
ground, like the sound of many waters, was enough to swallow
up all the powers of contemplation." [10]

By the middle of the 19th Century the sensationalism of the
camp meeting had greatly moderated, even while revivalism
continued to be an important element in American religious life.
The proliferation of evangelical sects and their popularity fostered the building of many small rural churches and reduced
the need for the large regional meetings. Indeed, each congregation often staged its own revival under the leadership of its own
preacher, thereby attracting fewer outsiders and non-believers,
and limiting attendance to those who already shared certain
convictions. Finally the greater circulation of religious literature,
not to mention the greater number of educated clergymen, had
the effect of standardizing church services and eliminating the
element of spontaneous participation.

In spatial terms the changes were no less evident: with the
coming of a permanent local preacher, the circuit rider, attached to no single community, fell out of favor, and the old
notion of church or parochial territoriality was revived, though
in less rigid form. Moreover, the very size and frequency of

camp meetings necessitated planning well in advance and careful preparation of the site; the former indifference to location was no longer possible. In 1834 a church paper proposed guidelines for the efficient organization of a camp meeting: both space and time were to be carefully structured. Meetings were to be held between the end of July and the end of September, presumably so as not to interfere with the work of planting and harvesting, and the site was to be one with "good water, dry ground, pleasant shade, agreeable woods for walking and recreation, timber for tentpoles and firewood, and pasturage for horses." It was finally recommended that camp meetings be less frequent, no more than two or three a year in a given district. The sermons were to be shorter, and the "sacraments to be administered according to the usual formulas, no extravagant exercises of any kind." [11]

The grove was on its way to becoming a combination summer resort and religious assembly place, and with the advent of the Chautauqua in the 1870s the tradition of the grove had undergone its final metamorphosis. The revolt against the inflexibility of liturgical time and against socially structured space had lasted a century, and already the carefully programmed service, the traditional sequence of ceremonies was beginning to return. The grove as a kind of non-environment, a space free of social or behavioral controls, was slowly acquiring a new structure: a correctly oriented platform for the preachers was prescribed, and an enclosure containing the "anxious bench" separated those intending to repent from the "mourners" or unconverted. Outside the assembly space itself special areas were set aside for family tents, and for single persons.

But no restoration is ever total, the pendulum never swings the entire distance. For all their renewed devotion to strict theology and their discovery of social causes, the Protestant churches learned the lesson that the emotional life of the individual could not be entirely ignored; the religious impulse was never again content with the highly structured space. The outdoor service, even the grove itself, reminded Americans that there was an escape from spaces imposing behavioral and social regimentation.

Revivals and new forms of piety continue to recur, and, whenever the existing spatial order proves too restrictive, new sacred groves or their equivalent will be discovered and used. Each such episode will reveal the link which has always existed between various forms of religious belief and the manner in which space and time are perceived.

The Necessity for Ruins

Not long ago Mr. Dillon Ripley of the Smithsonian's Museum of History and Technology happily announced the acquisition of the armchairs used by Archie Bunker and his wife Edith in the TV serial, "All in the Family."

The price was not mentioned, but commentators went out of their way to say pleasant things about the event. I have never liked the program, so I failed to share their enthusiasm. The Smithsonian, as I understand it, collects objects not only important in themselves — like the first typewriter, the first bicycle, Lindbergh's *Spirit of Saint Louis,* but also objects having some historical association, like the dresses worn by the wives of Presidents at inaugural balls. Under which heading did the Bunkers' two armchairs belong? Did Mr. Ripley suppose that a visitor to the Museum in the year (say) 2079 would find the armchairs inspiring to look at?

I am quite unable to guess; but as I look around the contemporary American scene I am puzzled by what seems generally to pass for a historical object or a monument. We admire and try to collect things not so much for their beauty or value as for their association with a phase of our past; and that is understandable, every generation has done the same. But with us the association seems to be not with our politically historical past, but with a kind of private vernacular past — what we cherish are mementos of a bygone daily existence without a definite date. Archie Bunker's armchair will recall — at least to the present generation — not only the many hours agreeably spent watching television, but also the environment, the setting, of a popular program, though not necessarily the program itself.

Much of our enthusiasm for historical preservation seems to

be prompted by the same instinct: history means less the record of significant events and people than the preservation of reminders of a bygone domestic existence and its environment.

What interests me is how this novel interpretation of history carries over from the museum or private collection into the wider rural and urban landscape. Anyone who travels through the United States must, I think, be aware of the widespread delight in what we can call reconstructed historical environments. Even in small and comparatively new communities there are groups eagerly organizing to save and restore old buildings and old neighborhoods and to have them registered as landmarks. But, in addition to these more or less legitimate examples of public piety, we run across numerous examples of Colonial Villages and Pioneer Villages and Frontier Villages and Army Posts which are in fact brand-new, and which we can visit for two dollars; the price allows us to watch the scheduled Indian raid or the stagecoach holdup or the noonday shootout.

There is hardly an enterprising town located on the more popular tourist routes that does not have some kind of reconstructed historical environment. Some are reasonably conscientious attempts at reconstruction; some of them are entirely make-believe. Fort Worth, which has an abandoned and decaying downtown stockyard area dating from the 1920s, is restoring it in the style of the 1870s. Another town in Texas, worried that a new bypass would ruin Main Street businesses, redecorated itself as a town of the 1890s and went into costume — every man, woman and child. Near where I live in New Mexico is a brand-new 18th Century Spanish Colonial village, with 18th Century harvest festivals and folkdances, that is hoping to achieve landmark status.

It is easy to expose and make fun of synthetic villages and roadside museums of junk from the recent past, just as it is easy to deplore Mr. Ripley's action in acquiring the Bunkers' chairs, just as it is easy to point out that much contemporary urban restoration is little more than a ploy to boost real estate values, or a way of keeping out undesirable neighbors. But the American public is not so gullible as we sometimes suppose, and it is not always easy to discern the motive behind the restoration.

There are examples which are in fact cultural achievements, contributions to our national heritage, and even the simplest of the reconstructed historical environments often betrays a respect for our past. People of intelligence and discernment admire not only Williamsburg and Sturbridge Village, but Old Town Albuquerque and Disneyland. The best explanation I can find for the nation-wide popularity of these environments is that they appeal to a radically new concept of history and of the meaning of history, and that they represent a radically new concept of the monument.

A traditional monument, as the origin of the word indicates, is an object which is supposed to remind us of something important. That is to say it exists to put people in mind of some obligation that they have incurred: a great public figure, a great public event, a great public declaration which the group had pledged itself to honor.

A monument can incidentally be a work of art or a public facility; it can even give pleasure. But those are secondary characteristics. A monument can be nothing more than a rough stone, a fragment of ruined wall as at Jerusalem, a tree, or a cross. Its sanctity is not a matter of beauty or of use or of age; it is venerated not as a work of art or as an antique, but as an echo from the remote past suddenly become present and actual. One of the most impressive modern monuments is the ruined church which stands in the center of the busiest part of West Berlin. It is an enormous ruin, without grace or picturesqueness, but for that very reason it provides a startling reminder of World War II, and is a monument whose message is not easy to forget. But there are in this country political monuments which have the same quality of vividly reminding us of an event or a person. The monument near the bridge at Concord, Massachusetts, is such a one, and I think the arch at St. Louis is another. I am speaking not of their esthetic quality, but of their power to remind, to recall something specific.

We can best understand the impact of the traditional monument by comparing it with that second yellow notice the telephone company sends out when we have forgotten to pay our bill. Our response is not to admire the phraseology of the notice or to dreamily recall the pleasant long-distance conversations of two or three months ago. We reach for our checkbook, angrily perhaps, in order to discharge the obligation and avoid future trouble.

It is obvious that monuments of this hortatory sort are likely to be numerous in any landscape where the inhabitants share a strong sense of a religious or political past, and moreover are concerned with their beginnings. That is why every new revolutionary social order, anxious to establish its image and acquire public support, produces many commemorative monuments and symbols and public celebrations. That is what we see in the Soviet Union or China or Cuba — or for that matter in Nazi Germany: a proliferation of public symbols of all sorts, not to please the public but to remind it of what it should believe and how it is to act.

That was the case when this country was young; a monument to the Revolution was erected as early as 1796 in Lexington, an obelisk, and for the next half century patriotic monuments and celebrations enlivened the landscape. Even place names helped remind Americans of our political traditions. A typical commemoration occurred in the 1830s when a monument was erected to the mother of George Washington at Mount Vernon. President Jackson and his cabinet came by steamer from Washington; there were cannon salutes, a military parade, poems were recited, and a large crowd was present. We can imagine what we would hear today if the mother of a President were being honored: many touching personal details, sentimentality about motherhood, and the devotion of the son. But in the 1830s the tone was entirely different. The purpose of the occasion was to remind the public of a great figure from the past. The chief orator had this to say: "If we look to the pages of history, or survey the earth we see that monuments have, in every age and every clime marked those spots distinguished by the happening of some great event, or risen as memorials of the once active virtues of departed worth.... Thus monuments are lasting incentives, to those who view them, to imitate the virtues they commemorate, and attain, by their life and spirit, glory and honor." President Jackson also made a speech, but no one made personal reference to Mary Washington.

When I was in school we had to read Webster's Bunker Hill oration, and Lincoln's Gettysburg Address. Both deal with monuments, and the Gettysburg Address is the most eloquent expression we can find of the classic point of view. The ostensible purpose of the Address was to dedicate a small graveyard where the remains of Northern soldiers were buried; but it can be read as a concise and beautiful description of what a monument means and how we should respond to it in our thoughts and actions.

Let me condense the passage which refers to the purpose of the gathering. "We are met to dedicate a portion of that [great battle-] field as the final resting place for those who here gave their lives that that nation might live. . . . It is for us, the living, rather, to be dedicated here to the unfinished work which they who fought here have thus far so nobly advanced. It is rather for us to be here dedicated to the great task remaining before us. . . ." Here in a few words the purpose of the monument is indicated: on a specific occasion a contract was entered into, a covenant was made, and the monument is to remind us of that contract. The monument, in short, is a guide to the future: just as it confers a kind of immortality on the dead, it determines our actions in the years to come.

For centuries that is what monuments and feast days had been for: to remind us of obligations, religious or political, and to keep us on the beaten path, loyal to tradition. Yet even as Lincoln was speaking, a new philosophy of history and the meaning of history was taking form among Americans.

No sooner was the Civil War at an end than there was a widespread desire to declare the Gettysburg battlefield a monument. This was something unheard of: an immense, populated landscape of thousands of acres of fields and roads and farmhouses becoming a monument to an event which had taken place there. It was in effect a reconstruction of the environment. It was no longer a reminder, it no longer told us what to do; it simply explained the battle. I do not mean to say that this battlefield as a monument is not extremely impressive; I merely suggest that it is not a monument in the traditional hortatory sense.

One reason for this change was that the American public no longer thought in terms of heroes, of the generals who had commanded the two armies as the only individuals deserving to be honored. There were tens of thousands of soldiers, many of them volunteers, who had fought and died and deserved a collective monument.

The history of American monumental art deserves to be studied, if only because it represents a very radical change in public attitudes. The most familiar expression of that change is the Civil War memorial we see in almost every American town. Some are elaborate, with many allegories, but the average memorial is a statue not of a local hero or of a famous commander, it is simply a statue of a Civil War soldier in uniform, with his rifle. It is an anonymous figure, a statue to what was literally an unknown soldier.

It would be interesting to know more about the origin of this simple but very effective memorial. It seems to have been well received, and before long America put up more monuments and statues to other anonymous figures — to men and women who had no specific accomplishment to their credit and who were identified with no outstanding event, but whom the American public was fond of, because they had been part of everyday existence. Probably the first was the statue of the anonymous Minute Man, by D. C. French, erected on the Lexington Green in 1876. We have all seen other examples: the anonymous Cowboy, the anonymous Newsboy, the anonymous Gloucester Fisherman. In the town of Enterprise, Alabama, there is a statue to the anonymous Boll Weevil. What is the purpose of these monuments? They do not remind us of any obligation, they suggest no particular line of conduct. They dignify certain obscure persons who had been useful and picturesque members of society, and to that extent express a very decent impulse. But I think there is more than that: I think this kind of monument is celebrating a different past, not the past which history books describe, but a vernacular past, a golden age where there are no dates or names, simply a sense of the way it *used to be,* history as the chronicle of everyday existence.

It is more than coincidence that at the same period — the last decades of the 19th Century — the average American public building began to lose some of its monumental, palatial quality. It is hard for us to see those florid courthouses and post offices and city halls as even remotely functional in design. But evidently people of the time sensed a change. Leopold Eidlitz, a celebrated American architect, the designer of the New York State Capitol, wrote more than eighty years ago: "We are busy in improving the material conditions of mankind and are apt to look upon ethical relations not so much as paramount in themselves but as adjuncts to material well-being. The priest and the soldier no longer govern the world. They are relegated to positions of servants of the people, and the merchant, the manufacturer, the builder of railroads and ships ... have taken the place of kings, bishops, and generals.... The majority of buildings which command the attention and services of the architect at the present time and in this country are strictly business buildings ... railroad stations, insurance and office buildings, stores and new offices.... Of course we build courts of justice and capitols; they ... represent vital social and political ideas.... But these ideas have been deprived of their poetry.... A judge no longer performs the functions inherent in his office in the past, he has sunk down into a referee who decides upon the cogency of contending lawyers.... Hence it is a fact that a courtroom is nothing more than a convenient apartment for legal discussion and a number of such apartments are habitually packed into a rectangular structure which can in no way be distinguished from surrounding business buildings." [1]

Eidlitz was saying that we no longer had the traditional heroes to honor, or the traditional kind of leaders; that public life was no longer ruled by traditional religious or political principles, and that private decisions had become the important ones.

Quite possibly he was right, even though many more statues to heroes were erected after his day. But they have become less and less popular. Over the last decades public scandals and

reappraisals of figures from the past have shown us that many
heroes and many events did not deserve to be celebrated, and
at the same time we have developed a lively interest in the
common man and his contribution to American history; indeed
his way of living and working and celebrating inspired many
of those historical restoration projects I mentioned earlier.

But something more than disillusionment with established
heroes accounts for the change in our attitude toward monuments, and one of the most revealing episodes in recent history
occurred a few decades ago when there was a question of
honoring Thomas Jefferson and later of honoring Franklin
Delano Roosevelt. At the time it was generally agreed that each
of them deserved a monument in Washington. But the debate
as to the *kind* of monument revealed that few had any clear
idea of the traditional monument or of the purpose it served.
Artists and critics argued as to the appropriateness of each style:
classical or contemporary? Simple or ornate? There were
liberals who said (as they always say on such occasions), why
spend so much on a pretentious building with no practical use
when the same amount of money could provide several places
of public recreation? And most significantly a number of prom-
inent architects and designers publicly admitted that they did
not know *how* to design a monument. They were not ashamed
of this deficiency; on the contrary, they offered it as evidence
that they were down-to-earth, practical men, impatient with
worn-out tradition.

The final proposals were either open-air environments —
places where the public could wander, sit down, eat lunch, and
relax — or vast displays of the writings and utterances of the
two heroes, great tablets where quotations were inscribed in
letters two feet high. I am no sort of architectural critic, but I
am inclined to believe that when a designer relies on inscrip-
tions to make his point he is tacitly admitting artistic incom-
petence.

Since that time, more than twenty years ago, it appears that
the average American community has pretty well abandoned
the traditional monument and has found new ways of celebrating past events. The manner in which we commemorated the

Bicentennial is strong evidence. Let me try to illustrate the
change by contrasting the traditional — one might almost say
the Latin — attitude with our own.

The Latin community or nation decides to commemorate
the hundredth anniversary of the birth of President X. After
long debate it chooses as the appropriate day the anniversary
of the president's assassination. On that date it inaugurates a
splendid marble shaft supporting a bronze statue of President X
holding in one hand a bronze scroll labelled "Constitution of
1953." The shaft is adorned with allegorical statues of Industry,
Agriculture, Education, and Social Welfare. There is a company of soldiers in dress uniform, a formal parade up the
Avenue of the 27 of July (the date of the president's birth), and
several speeches recounting the hero's accomplishments with
emphasis on the wisdom of following his policies. The public
sings the national anthem. That afternoon a model housing
development — named President X Village — is inaugurated,
and a new political party is formed, dedicated to keeping alive
the principles of President X.

But how do we celebrate history in the U.S.A.? The town
of Centerville suddenly realizes that it is approximately one
hundred and fifty years old. (No one knows the year when the
first settler arrived, or who he was.) A mass meeting is held
in the high school gym to discuss how to celebrate the event. It
is finally agreed that it would be nice to feature the arrival of
the first train, sometime in the 1850s, and the Indian raid of
1847, and at the same celebration to inaugurate the new senior
citizen housing project. On a lighter tone it is suggested that
all the men in Centerville grow beards.

So Centerville sets to work. Hitching posts are installed along
one block of Main Street, gas lights substituted for electricity,
the front of the town hall is restored to its original 1890 appearance. In the window of the drugstore old prescription
ledgers are displayed; the library shows a collection of ancient
photographs. Finally a log cabin is built in the new Pioneer
Memorial Park near the river on the outskirts of town; it is
eventually to be used and maintained by the Boy Scouts. On
the 4th of July there is a parade of antique automobiles, a

barbecue in the new park, followed by square dancing with everyone in costume, though of no particular period. The town historian reads an amusing poem about the good old days, bringing in as many local names as he can.

The celebration is pronounced a great success. Centerville puts up a large sign on the highway saying "Welcome to Centerville — Historical Pioneer Village."

The comparison is not much exaggerated; each celebration indicates a distinct approach not only to monuments but to history. The Latin version — the one we used to prefer — sees the past as highly structured, highly political in the real meaning of that word. Past and present are linked by a contract, a covenant between the people and their leaders, and this covenant is given visible form in monuments and a temporal form in a series of scheduled holidays and days of commemoration. The present is the continuation, the re-enactment of the past, modified of course by intervening events, but the community is constantly reminded of its original identity and its ancient pledges. The emphasis is on the continuity of history.

On the other hand the contemporary American celebration suggests that the past is a remote, ill-defined period or environment when a kind of golden age prevailed, when society had an innocence and a simplicity that we have since lost; a period usually referred to as The Old Days, or as (Eliade calls it) *in illo tempore* — in those days — a time without significant events, and a landscape without monuments.

Both points of view celebrate the past and seek to make it a part of daily life. No phrases are more common in America than "safeguarding our heritage" or "keeping alive our cherished traditions"; but it is clear, I think, that most of us have ceased to see the basis of our historical existence as a sequence of political events: Revolution, Declaration of Independence, Constitution, Civil War. I live in a town which with some justification is known as the most historic area in the West. It dates from the early 17th Century. There are, however, only two monuments in the region to individuals, and I doubt if one resident out of ten could identify three dates in the town's

history. And yet there never was such a place for restoration
and preservation and the cult of the old days as Santa Fe.

I confess that I find myself entirely out of sympathy with this
romanticization of history, but the question remains: why do so
many people derive pleasure and even inspiration from the deliberate re-building or invention of historical environments, even
when they recognize the artificiality of most of these? Is it simply nostalgia, is it simply a touristic instinct in search of the
unusual, or does it have a deeper significance? I know of no
easy answer, but one answer, like the answer to so many questions related to the environment and how we perceive it, lies in
different religious attitudes.

Several years ago, the geographer of religions, Erich Isaac,
wrote an article in *Landscape Magazine* entitled "The Impact
of Religions on the Landscape." Most geographers have discussed this topic largely in terms of orientation, sacred mountains, sacred wells, the taboo on certain plants and animals, and
so on. But Isaac had a different approach. In the article he described the landscape of a small, remote tribe in southern Rho-
desia, and noted the impact — or rather the lack of impact —
of religious practices and beliefs on the environment. He came
to the following conclusions: religions which conceive of the
creation of the world as marking the beginning of human existence and human society have a much greater impact on the
landscape than religions which perceive the real beginning of
existence as deriving from a divine charter or covenant.[2] To
phrase it differently, Isaac said that a society which dates its
beginning from the very creation of the world, which sees itself
as the direct product of the cosmic plan, is likely to believe that
the way to achieve harmony with the environment is to transform — or restore — that environment in imitation of its original condition. We are familiar with the elaborate cosmic symbolism in the houses and towns and fields of the Dogon of
Africa, but the same kind of symbolism has existed in parts of
South America; and in China, if I understand it, the doctrine
of *feng-shui* is also essentially the celebration of an unchanging
cosmic order.

But this attitude is by no means universal. When a religion like Christianity or Judaism or Islam assumes that the true meaning of existence derives not from the beginning of the world but from some extraordinary event or revelation, from a covenant between man and the divinity, then that religion is concerned not with reproducing any cosmic symbolism on the landscape, it is concerned with man's keeping the terms of the covenant, with his obeying the divine law.

Can we translate these religious concepts into social concepts? Can we say that a society which sees itself as having had a definite political or legal origin — like the United States — with its own birthday and birth certificate and contract in the form of a semi-sacred Constitution, is likely to be attached to monuments or dates which are reminders of political covenants? But a society which sees itself as having slowly evolved, beginning with the very first settlements in its own environment, is more likely to celebrate its legendary, half-forgotten origins in the landscape; it looks back not to a specific event, but to a golden age when it was at one with its environment.

The question of course is why and when did Americans abandon the old covenant approach to their history and take on an evolutionary approach? That is for historians to explain, but I can only suggest that such shifts are not rare, and that every culture, even the most archaic, shows signs of overlapping or contradictory interpretations of existence. The evidence suggests that around the middle of the last century America began to think of itself as a unique society which had evolved over two centuries of time — a notion in line with other theories of evolution becoming widespread in that period.

And this is more or less the way we see ourselves now: as a society which has grown and expanded over most of a continent, a kind of elemental force. There are certainly traits in our present attitude toward our history — and toward monuments and holidays — that suggest that there is something in common between our enthusiasm for restored (or invented) historical environments and that other concept of the origin of existence. It is probably not necessary to point to the current movement to preserve wilderness or natural areas as fragments of what we might call the original design of creation. The instinct behind the drive is very similar to that which inspires our architectural restorations: to restore as much as possible the *original* aspect of the landscape. It is perfectly true that to restore part of a town to its mid–19th Century appearance is not in fact to restore it to its original form. But anthropologists tell us that, in the thought of most peoples, primal time — the golden age, that is to say — begins precisely where active memory ends — thus about the time of one's great-grandfather. Perhaps this accounts for our present fascination with the 1870s and 1880s. That was in fact a period of great change, but it is now remote enough to be perceived as part of the old days and in consequence to be the theme of countless small town restorations.

When we think of the immense changes still being made by the growth of population and by technology in the American landscape it seems absurd to say that we are at the same time reproducing or restoring the *original* landscape, the image of creation. But even in the case of the Dogon and similar societies the area transformed in a symbolic manner was very small, only a few significant spots were given symbolic treatment. The same is true with us. Even so, over the last years a vast number of historical environments have come into being: outdoor museums, roadside museums, wilderness areas, historic zones and neighborhoods; and we should not overlook the new and widespread interest in the industrial landscape — 19th Century mills and factories and railroad stations and bridges and mines. There is even a society of commercial archeology which seeks to preserve old gas stations and storefronts.

It seems clear that the whole preservation and restoration movement is much more than a means of promoting tourism or a sentimentalizing over an obscure part of the past — though it is also both of those things. We are learning to see it as a new (or recently rediscovered) interpretation of history. It sees history not as a continuity but as a dramatic discontinuity, a kind of cosmic drama. First there is that golden age, the time of harmonious beginnings. Then ensues a period when the old days are forgotten and the golden age falls into neglect. Finally comes a time when we rediscover and seek to restore the world around us to something like its former beauty.

But there has to be that interval of neglect, there has to be discontinuity; it is religiously and artistically essential. That is what I mean when I refer to the necessity for ruins: ruins provide the incentive for restoration, and for a return to origins. There has to be (in our new concept of history) an interim of death or rejection before there can be renewal and reform. The old order has to die before there can be a born-again landscape. Many of us know the joy and excitement not so much of creating the new as of redeeming what has been neglected, and this excitement is particularly strong when the original condition is seen as holy or beautiful. The old farmhouse has to decay before we can restore it and lead an alternative life style in the country; the landscape has to be plundered and stripped before we can restore the natural ecosystem; the neighborhood has to be a slum before we can rediscover it and gentrify it. That is how we reproduce the cosmic scheme and correct history.

Are we perhaps trying to re-enact some ancient myth of birth, death, and redemption? I sometimes think I see the logical consequences: the return of a kind of pageantry or ritual in connection with many of these new historical shrines. The parade as an art form or as a political symbol is all but dead. Like the political monument it has ceased to have any symbolical impact. But a kind of historical, theatrical make-believe is becoming increasingly popular; not only the noonday shootouts and other roadside attractions, but costumed guides in historical show places, candlelight concerts of period music, historically accurate dinners and feasts, re-enactments of historic episodes are gradually changing the new reconstructed environments into scenes of unreality, places where we can briefly relive the golden age and be purged of historical guilt. The past is brought back in all its richness. There is no lesson to learn, no covenant to honor; we are charmed into a state of innocence and become part of the environment. History ceases to exist.

The Domestication of the Garage

To be interested in the popular culture of contemporary America is to be interested in our popular architecture; the architecture of those buildings in which we live or work or enjoy ourselves. They are not only an important part of our everyday environment, they also reveal in their design and evolution much about our values and how we adjust to the surrounding world.

That is why the study of vernacular (as opposed to "polite") architecture is more and more appreciated as a source of fresh insights into the social history of a period or a people. The question is (and always has been) which architectural forms are we to choose? Until about a century ago, little uncertainty existed; historians and cultural geographers told us that vernacular architecture meant the dwelling and its dependencies, public works such as bridges and mills and fortifications, and even sometimes the church. These were the products of craftsmen, members of a predominantly rural or pre-technological society, using traditional methods and locally available materials and working with practical ends in view. Folk or vernacular architecture was thus largely interpreted in terms of structure and (by extension) in terms of the exploitation of local natural resources.

But since the 19th Century there have been many changes; we have learned to see the dwelling as a much more complicated thing, and the architectural scene has immensely expanded. Innumerable new forms have evolved, not only in our public existence — such as the factory, the shopping center, the gas station, and so on — but in our private lives as well. The home has been radically changed by the elimination of certain spaces and by the addition of new spaces.

The garage is a case in point. How is this particular feature — now almost essential to the family dwelling — to be interpreted in traditional vernacular terms? Is it to be thought of as the product of the craftsman? Is it somehow to be related to the economic function of the dwelling? Are we to try to establish regional or ethnic variations? Or must we reject the garage altogether? On the other hand, should we perhaps work toward a new definition of vernacular architecture that would *include* the garage?

The Romantic Garage. The word is of French origin, of course, and means more or less a storage space. It is related to the English *ware* as in warehouse, and we could easily have devised an appropriate term such as *warage*. But our borrowing from the French was an indication of the exotic (not to say, expensive) nature of early automobile culture. Current descriptions of the introduction of the automobile, with their exaggerated emphasis on breakneck races and the contributions of small mechanics, do not give us a true idea of the original status of the automobile in this country. To most of its owners at the turn of the century it was a pleasure vehicle and a toy, costly, exciting, and of extraordinary elegance: gleaming with brass and rich enamel, its form (even then) suggestive of power and speed. For controlling and maintaining this complicated machine it was wise to engage a specialist — who (again) was given a French name, *chauffeur,* meaning fireman, and who, because of his daring, his mechanical genius, and his style, had a special status. In *Man and Superman,* Henry Straker, Tanner's chauffeur, was the object of respect and an uneasy admiration from his employer. Shaw suggests that he represented the male counterpart of the New Woman, someone disdainful of traditional social views and in touch with future realities.

The housing of this valuable plaything, and of the chauffeur as well, was a matter of importance. In town the problem was solved by the availability of livery stables and improvised storage spaces where rentals, even in the first decade of the century, were likely to be as high as fifty dollars a month. But automobile owners who lived in the suburbs or the country depended on the stable or coach house. For sanitary reasons this was usually isolated at some distance from the dwelling, in the rear of the grounds — an arrangement which seemed suitable for the automobile as well, for who knew what might not happen if the gasoline fumes made contact with the kitchen stove? Part of the stable became what was briefly called the *motor house,* and the chauffeur had his lodgings in a room overhead.

Architects were even engaged by the well-to-do to design combination stables, carriage houses, and garages; in 1911 Frank Lloyd Wright produced a monumental example on a suburban Chicago estate. Nevertheless the solution proved impractical. Acids emanating from the stables repeatedly tarnished the brass trim on the cars and even threatened to damage the paint. Keeping the cars clean and polished called for a special washing area, and no doubt the horses and their attendants were likewise inconvenienced. So at an early date the single-purpose garage emerged as an autonomous, more or less self-sufficient, building type, stylishly functional. In 1906 *House Beautiful* published a spread of some of the more imposing specimens — Colonial, Tudor, Craftsman, as the case might be. Few subsequent designs surpassed them in size and dignity. A second story accommodated the chauffeur; the storage space itself was large, well-lighted, and efficiently planned, often with a turntable (to eliminate having to back out), an overhead hoist, and a pit. This last feature disappeared when cars were designed to give access to the motor from under the hood instead of underneath.

There are suggestions in the brief literature on garage design of the period that architects enjoyed the challenge of producing strictly utilitarian interiors which would serve as settings for the engineered beauty of the automobile and the spit-and-polish work of the chauffeur; there seems to have flourished (not for very long) a kind of Machine Age esthetic of the garage.

But physically as well as psychologically the garage remained isolated from the dwelling: at the end of a long driveway behind the house, or hidden by a wall. Only after the chauffeur had cranked the motor into action, tested the sparkplugs and

the tension of the leather fan belt, checked the oil and poured in
a gallon or two of gasoline did the car, figuratively speaking,
join the family. Outside the front door ensued the ritual of pull-
ing on gauntlets, adjusting veils and goggles and lap-robes
(while the automobile quivered restlessly), and finally waving
goodbye. There was an early tendency — happily *long since*
overcome but natural enough in those adventurous days — to
show off while driving. Various periodicals dealing with country or suburban life urged their readers to behave with dignity
on the highway. In 1909, *House and Garden* cautioned: "No
toes peeping over the body of the tonneau or feet resting on
the dashboard or arms or wraps hanging over the sides, smok-
ing limited to one person, preferably not the driver. Whistles,
bells, quacking novelties and sirens seem out of place in town
although in the country they may be used to advantage....
Among the purely ornamental novelties of motordom the small
gilt figure of an eagle has almost entirely monopolized the place
on top of the radiator.... This is a very pretty custom if the
figure be small, and quite patriotic where the bill holds a narrow
ribbon of the national colors."

There exists a body of attractive if ephemeral writing —
mostly novels and brief travel accounts — dealing with the early
days of the car and the romance of driving. *The Wind in the
Willows* is perhaps the only title to have survived.

The Practical Garage. In the meantime a much more prosaic
automobile culture, and a much more popular one, was emerging among middle class Americans. Entirely excluded from the
wealthy world of imported pleasure cars and know-it-all chauf-
feurs, the world of automotive sport, hundreds of thousands and
eventually millions of car owners learned to value their automobiles as an increasingly important element in their everyday
existence, for pleasure of course, but also for the daily domestic
routine and for work. The first Americans to see the car in these
terms were probably farmers and country doctors; for them it
was a vehicle for emergencies. But it was not long before many
others whose work called for mobility — traveling salesmen and
agents, repair and service and delivery men — used the automo-

bile in their work, made their own repairs, and aspired to nothing more than models which were inexpensive and reliable.

And consequently a very different kind of garage came into existence. The small portable or prefabricated item, scarcely larger than the car itself, was for many working owners the practical answer. In closely built-up neighborhoods in most American cities the service alley, beginning at about the time of World War I, was lined with these boxlike structures. The dimensions of the average American city lot — 25 feet by 100 — precluded the building of any garage next to the dwelling itself; and as a result the home garage for the freestanding dwelling was relegated to the rear of the lot. Two parallel cement pathways provided a lane from garage door to curb. It was an unsightly arrangement, and it had the effect of completing the ruin of the backyard. This small private area had rarely been attractive: surrounded by a high wooden wall, dominated by the revolving clothesline, a convenient place to put the trashcan, the ashes from the furnace, and the doghouse, it had become a source of shame, and the advent of the garage concluded its disgrace.

Those days, a half century ago, after the car had become popular but before the garage had been assimilated into the dwelling, can perhaps be thought of as a period of transition between the concept of the home as the locus of high-minded educational and hygienic endeavor and the present concept of the home as a place for recreation and fun. Yet it is hard to find any evidence that architects or planners recognized the existence of the family automobile or of the problems it created. It was only in 1916 that city planners began to take the automobile into account even in the discussion of urban transportation.[1] Many well-intentioned designs for moderately priced houses were published during the twenties and not a few of them received awards; but although a number of them included maids' rooms, scarcely one of them thought of the garage or even of overnight parking space. Radburn, in New Jersey, designed in 1928, gives perhaps the first sign we have of awareness of the garage as an essential adjunct to the dwelling — and even there it was segregated and hidden from view.

What one *does* find at this time, however, are occasional examples of relatively expensive architect-designed suburban dwellings — especially in California — where the garage is attached to the house. This innovation became noticeable in the thirties. Yet this purpose seems to have been primarily esthetic: to heighten the interest of the architectural composition, to produce striking or picturesque masses or roof lines. And the proof of this is that the garage rarely if ever communicated directly with the house. It remained functionally isolated from the domestic establishment, as if the vehicle it contained were little more than an occasional convenience having no bearing on the way life was lived. In 1939 a columnist in a shelter magazine remarked: "You can't have failed to notice how in all the new home plans the family garage is 'tied in' with the house if the architect can possibly manage it. But the old garages, plunked down on one side of the house, halfway back in the garden, their doors yawning to the street, their walls bare, and their angular lines unsoftened by shrubbery — they *are* ugly."

The Family Garage. Two decades later, after World War II, the whole garage scene had undergone a radical change. Not only was the garage in the average detached dwelling thoroughly integrated into the street façade of the house — to the point where its wide doors served to balance the picture window so popular in the fifties — it was *internally* integrated. A conveniently placed door led either into the kitchen or into what is known among home builders as the *mud room* — a kind of decompression chamber for members of the family returning from work or school. Furthermore, the garage itself had greatly expanded, becoming spacious enough to accommodate not only two cars, but a deep freeze, a washer and dryer, and even a hot-water unit and a hobby work bench — to say nothing of broken lawn furniture, skis, and tangles of garden hose. In short, it had become thoroughly domesticated, an integral part of home life and the routine of work and play. On its wide concrete apron — often occupying a third of the frontage — the family car was washed and polished every Sunday, and on weekday afternoons the young of the family shot basketballs. What the stork's nest

on the chimney of the northern European home traditionally
signified, the basketball backstop over the garage door signified
for the American home: a child-oriented domesticity.

How are we to account for this relatively abrupt transformation? We can perhaps enumerate some of the external forces —
forces not originating within the family itself — which were at
work between the Depression and the end of World War II,
though it would be impossible to say which of these was the
most important in changing the whole form of the middle class
American home. For one thing, cars increased in width and
length and outgrew the old backyard garage and the narrow
driveway leading to it. Then the boom in suburban and tract-
house building produced, in many outlying communities, house-
lots with a wider frontage, and this of course allowed for a
garage on the street. Families acquired two cars and even three;
the decline in public transportation and the growth of urban
and suburban distances meant that two cars were a necessity for
many families of moderate income — one for work and one for
household errands and transporting the children. A decrease in
home delivery services had two very different consequences: the
dwelling had to become more self-sufficient (acquiring a washer
and dryer and deep freeze) and more trips were called for, more
loads had to be brought home — and deposited in the garage.

In all of these changes or adjustments in the spatial organization of the American home the garage has of course played a
most important role. And since the garage was designed and
provided by the builder, it might be said (and often *is* said by
critics) that the contemporary house is entirely the creation of
the housing industry, therefore not vernacular in the accepted
meaning of the word.

But this verdict disregards the *internal* changes — the changes
which the occupants themselves have produced or inspired. For
it is easy to establish that many shifts in domestic values and
objectives took place *before* the homebuilders altered their designs. Only one of these internal changes can be mentioned
here: the advent, sometime in the late thirties, of the concept of
the home as a place for recreation and entertainment. Long
before mass-produced housing recognized this tendency and be-

gan to introduce festive elements, American families were transforming the basement (where the oil burner had replaced the
coal furnace) into a rumpus room or game room or activities
room. Long before the advent of colorful kitchens with Mediterranean décor, Americans were busily disguising the bleak white
antiseptic surface of the scientific kitchen.

There is in fact scarcely a space in the modern American
dwelling that owners themselves have not transformed in keeping with this new image. Even the backyard, freed of its clothesline and rubbish and of the obsolete garage, became a recreation
area well before homebuilders saw its potential charm. Barbecue pit, plastic wading pool, power lawnmower, all antedate the
developers' concept of Holiday Homesteads. And the garage as
a family center half outdoors, part work area, part play area, is
also a family invention, not the invention of designers.

The contribution of the homebuilder to the promotion of the
leisure-oriented home has certainly been important, but it has
chiefly been a matter of sensing shifts in taste and giving them a
saleable form. It is only lately, for instance, that the housing industry has seen what the garage has come to signify. The *Practical Builder* in 1968 proposed the *three-car* garage. The added
massiveness, the magazine suggested, would make for a more
impressive house and the three garage doors would imply three
cars and a corresponding larger income. Surely these are very
out-of-date concepts, long since abandoned by the prospective
homeowner! And the magazine added (as if it had made a
startling discovery) that the extra space could be put to use for
storing pleasure boats, for the pursuit of hobbies, for a play area
on rainy days. But in scores of housing developments we had
already acted on the suggestions; it is we who design or rede-
sign our homes, the homebuilders merely provide their
structure.

Just as the builders were a good decade behind the times in
realizing the importance of the garage in the twenties and thirties, they have been behind the times in seeing that the multi-
purpose garage has become an integral part of the new leisure-
oriented dwelling. There is nothing blameworthy in this; the
housing industry has not claimed to do more than satisfy well

established needs, though it does not always do this very well. But the mass homebuilder has in a sense come up with a good working definition of middle class architecture: the visible result of a confrontation between the aspirations of the occupying family and economic and social realities. There is no permanent solution to the conflict; there never will be. That is why we will go on evolving new kinds of vernacular architecture; that is why the contemporary American dwelling with its all-purpose garage is an authentic example of what vernacular means.

By Way of Conclusion:
How to Study the Landscape

AS I HAVE MENTIONED EARLIER, for a number of years I taught an undergraduate course at Harvard and at Berkeley that was called "The History of the American Cultural Landscape." It dealt with such commonplace things as fences and roads and barns, the design of factories and office buildings, the layout of towns and farms and graveyards and parks and houses, and toward the end of the course I talked about the superhighway and the strip and certain new kinds of sports which I referred to as psychedelic. Throughout the course I showed a good many slides, and each student had to write a term paper on some aspect of the contemporary American landscape.

Slide shows are popular in the classroom, and though my slides were poor in quality, they were of familiar, everyday objects and places, and that, I suspect, was the principal reason for the success of the course. Of necessity much college education deals with ideas and theories and is based on reading and study, and so an undergraduate course which required no preliminary experience, which discussed the contemporary world and how it had evolved over the past two centuries, and which was not overly critical of American culture — such a course was probably welcome as a relief, or at least as a change.

It is the accepted European procedure, as I understand it, to start exposing a line of thought by first enunciating a few guiding principles and then providing examples, and this is the method followed by many American professors. But the traditional Anglo-Saxon procedure is the opposite: it states the facts, provides examples, and only at the end presumes to draw conclusions. This was my approach and I found it satisfactory, if for no other reason than that I had no clear-cut conclusions or generalizations to offer. I had traveled enough in the United States to know the country well, and I had tried to familiarize myself with what can be called its vernacular history; and it was this experience which I undertook to pass on to the students. I confined my introductory remarks to such obvious statements as that a landscape (whether urban or rural) gradually took form when people moved into a place, did what they could to survive and prosper with the resources at hand, and that they soon organized themselves into a group for mutual help and protection and for celebration of one kind or another. I added that landscapes grew and changed and that they had a chronology that was often interesting to explore. This was followed by the display of a few slides illustrating change in certain familiar places.

So, the logical beginning of the course on the history of the American landscape, as I saw it, was a brief account of the arrival of the first settlers in a region — whether Virginia, New England or North Dakota. The settlers appeared on the scene, explored their surroundings, and then proceeded to make themselves at home. This is also how conventional history books begin. They give a description of the way the new community sets up certain basic institutions: for government, for defense, for communication with the outside world; the way it establishes a school and a church, and builds places to live and work in.

But the student of landscapes has another interest: how space is organized by the community. This means the drawing of a boundary, the efficient dividing up of the land among the several families, the providing of roads and a place of public assembly, and the setting aside of land for communal use. So, while the conventional historian prefers to date the birth of the community as a political entity from that moment when all gather together in a tent or under a tree and pass a number of solemn resolutions, the landscape student likes to call attention to another, equally significant moment — when the first line is scratched in the soil or the first blaze cut in a tree or the first stone marker is erected. These are those *Traces on the Rhodian Shore* that Clarence Glacken has described in his wonderful book. The event is no doubt trifling and soon forgotten, but how is a society, even a small pioneer society, to function, how is it to have form and a degree of permanence unless it has its own territory, unless it creates and occupies its own space?

No one has written with greater authority and insight on the subject of space than Professor Yi-Fu Tuan, and his book, *Space and Place,* continues to be the inspiration and guide of every landscape student. For the significance of space in landscape terms, the allotment of land for private or public use, is that it makes the social order visible. Space, even a small plot of ground, identifies the occupant and gives him status, and most important of all, it establishes lasting relationships. As the word itself suggests, a boundary is what binds us all together in a group, that which excludes the outsider or stranger. The boundary creates neighbors; it is the symbol of law and order and permanence. The network of boundaries, private as well as public, transforms an amorphous environment into a human landscape, and nothing more clearly shows some of the cherished values of a group than the manner in which they fix those boundaries, the manner in which they organize space. And, because these values change in the course of time, the organization of space also undergoes a change. That is one reason why the contemporary landscape is so different from that of even a hundred years ago.

The original layout of spaces is well worth studying, it seems to me, if only because it unconsciously reveals so much about the ideas of men and women who devised it. If I had to reconstruct my course, or if I were asked what I thought should be emphasized, I think I would say that the significance of boundaries and spatial divisions could hardly be overstressed. Few Americans, I discovered, have any notion of what the national grid system signifies in terms of political philosophy. We either criticize its monotony and its disregard of the lay of the land, or else we assume it was the product of real estate speculators. But as we should know, the grid system is, in fact, one of the most ambitious schemes in history for the orderly creation of landscapes, of small communities. When its scope and purpose are explained, I find that students are quick to respond, and from then on they are alert to other kinds of spatial organization — the careful distribution of land according to the merits of the family in colonial New England or the *laisser faire* procedure followed in the Oklahoma land rush. And what I find most satisfying is that some students even learn to appreciate the grandeur and beauty of the grid.

To talk about the grid means talking about fields and fences and roads and crossroads and school houses, and eventually it means talking about the grid in towns and cities. We have to backtrack and discuss the Philadelphia version of the grid and the Philadelphia way of naming streets versus the Southern grid and the Southern way of naming streets, and even the Mormon grid — more familiar in the West, of course, than elsewhere. And then there are several kinds of courthouse square, as Professor Price has told us; and while we are on the subject of spatial organization of the early American town, it is easy to discuss the unique qualities of the American addition or subdivision — which in the old days meant simply the selling of land, the house being built by the purchaser; whereas in Europe, the original landowner also built the houses and thereby created a distinct community or neighborhood. The grid system, at least during its early days, allowed for a wonderful flexibility in the use of space, and even a degree of interchangeability, for all lots, all blocks, all streets were of uniform dimensions and you could build what you liked, *where* you liked. A good illustration of how interchangeability was characteristic of the early, pre-industrial landscape was the popularity until about 1850 of the Greek revival style. It was considered equally appropriate for banks, courthouses, mansions, post offices, college buildings, and churches. Using slides, I had shown how versatile the style could be.

As will have been noted, it was the pre-industrial town that we discussed, the town which flourished before the factory and the railroad had invaded every part of the landscape, even though there was a water powered mill in the average town, and often there were steamboats on the river. But a pre-

industrial town can be a very complicated element in any landscape, and I long hesitated to discuss the urban scene before
discussing the rural scene. There were several reasons, however,
why I eventually thought the time had come. First of all, it is
one of the peculiarities of the United States, as Richard Wade
has pointed out, that in many regions towns came before
farms; towns as trading posts, as defense installations, as transfer points in river navigation, were often in existence long before the surrounding forest had been invaded by pioneer farmers. So it was the town which set the pace in the development of
the landscape, established forms and spaces. But another reason
for discussing the pre-industrial town was that it still represents
for most Americans the most picturesque and appealing aspect
of our past. The small town of that period is familiar in our
popular art and literature and folklore: the town with its central
square or marketplace, with its fairground and local academy or
college, its so-called block of offices on the main street, the First
Church with its graveyard where the first settlers are buried,
and the Greek revival façades along the tree-lined streets leading out to the open country. There is always the danger, in
dealing with that remote period, of lapsing into sentimental
antiquarianism, a glorification of the simpler ways of the early
Republic that many young people are very susceptible to. On
the other hand, since most students have an urban background,
they have an instinctive understanding of how to interpret the
town's spaces, and are often expert at discovering its style and
its search for order.

My final reason for discussing the town instead of the country
was this: the town, particularly the pre-industrial town, offers
the best material for studying the house or dwelling.

There is a school of cultural geographers which believes that
the dwelling is not only the most important element in the
landscape, but is the key to understanding all other elements in
the landscape: the social order, the economy, the natural resources, the history, and culture. It so happens that the dwelling
which these geographers usually have in mind is the European
farmhouse or farmstead — a combination under one roof of
residence, and storage, and work areas. In use and in design

and in materials, this farmhouse is closely attuned to the surrounding land, and is, in fact, a product of it. Few American farmhouses, however, resemble the farmhouses of the Old World. Most of them are designed and used as residences, pure and simple, and are essentially like the dwellings in the nearby town, inhabited by lawyers, and merchants, and clergymen. Indeed, our farmhouses are often copies of these urban counterparts. We ought to be cautious, then, in how we accept some of the European theories about the relationship between dwelling and landscape. A house in Juneau, Alaska, is much more likely to resemble a house in Shreveport, Louisiana, than an Eskimo dwelling a few hundred miles away. Perhaps we deplore this circumstance, but it is essential that we learn to live with it; and I can think of no better way for landscape studies to achieve academic respectability than for it to formulate a new and American way of defining housetypes based not on the 19th Century concern for regionalism, use of local materials, local craftsmanship, and local agriculture, but on thoroughly contemporary notions: the dwelling defined in terms of its longevity, of its relationship to work, to the family, to the community, and of its psychological relationship to the natural environment.

What makes an enterprise of this sort easier and at the same time more appropriate is that all students — and indeed all people — have an innate interest in houses. Whether they come from the city or the country, whether they live in a trailer or an apartment or a bungalow or a mansion, students, I have found, immediately respond to any discussion of the dwelling, its construction, its layout, its appearance, its many functions, and its evolution over the centuries. Like every other instructor, I have read many hundreds of term papers. In my case, they discussed some aspect of the contemporary landscape — usually the landscape of the small town or the farm countryside. Those which I found most enjoyable and most perceptive dealt with such modest topics as the front porch or the local Civil War monument, or with barns and roads. I enjoyed them not only for their content — they often revealed obscure historical information — but because they seemed to be based on childhood memories and family traditions. It was from such papers that

I learned about the complicated make-up of towns which to the outsider seemed entirely homogeneous: the nicknames for certain sections, certain streets and alleys, the location of all but invisible ethnic communities. The papers told of family customs, high school rituals, church festivities; they revealed half-forgotten farming practices and beliefs, and the existence of small gardens where plants unheard of in the region were grown, year after year. All this made for pleasant reading. But there were also papers — not many of them — that recorded everyday sensory experiences of the landscape: the sound of snow shovels after a blizzard, the smell of wet bathing suits, the sensation of walking barefoot on the hot pavement. A woman student from North Dakota wrote of her family driving each fall to the nearest town to see the autumn foliage in the streets and yards; out where she lived there were no trees. This kind of landscape perception is something no instructor can teach. We can only be grateful when it comes our way, and encourage students to record such fleeting memories as these, and share them. They often make a whole landscape, a whole season, vivid and unforgettable.

I have already mentioned it in passing and I will say it again for emphasis: this kind of landscape and landscape study is essentially preparatory. It deals with the rural or small town past, with an America which, except in a few isolated regions, has disappeared or changed beyond recognition. Why then, it will be asked, should we bother to study it? Why should we not follow the geographer's precedent, and simply acquaint ourselves with the current scene?

I can think of three good reasons for starting by examining the landscape of the early 19th Century and earlier. The studies provide the student with a better view of our vernacular history than Disneyland and its imitations do or than the student is likely to acquire from tendentious socio-economic texts. Second, it is an excellent and relatively painless way of learning about the purpose of landscape studies, for it deals with familiar, more or less simple archetypes. And third, we can only start to understand the contemporary landscape by knowing what we have rejected and what we have retained from the past. I doubt

if there is any other part of the modern world where the
contrast between the traditional landscape and the contemporary landscape is so easy to observe; where the two exist in
relative harmony, untroubled by class or race identification.

So there comes a day, usually around mid-term, when the
students are informed that we are about to embark on the study
of a landscape of a very different kind: the landscape which
began to emerge around the middle of the 19th Century and
which is now approaching full flower. It is popular to say that
we are in a period of transition — and it has been said, with
some justification, for the past hundred years. But the phrase
represents a kind of evasion, an unwillingness to recognize that
in many areas of our culture the final form can be discerned.
The notion of a kind of perpetual transition has the effect of
making us appraise many things in terms of a familiar past
instead of in terms of present-day realities. The widespread
belief that ours is a transitional landscape is a case in point: we
tend to see it not as it is, with its own unique character, but
as a degenerate version of the traditional landscape, and to see
its history as a long, drawn-out backsliding, the abandonment
of old values, old techniques, old institutions, with nothing
developing to take their place.

But a more sensible approach, it seems to me, is to try to
discover when some of its characteristics first made their appearance, rather than to dwell on the disappearance of
the old. The gradual obsolescence of the traditional multi-
purpose barn is not so important as the rise of a kind of farming
where no barn is needed, and all produce is trucked to a
local processing plant.

The discussion of the contemporary American landscape
should start with the transformation of a basic landscape
element: the piece of land or the farm. In the traditional order
of things, at least in the United States, the ideal was that the
family who owned the land also lived on it and worked it;
family status came from the relationship, and in fact many
colonial statutes and even the Homestead Act of 1862 stipulated
that a dwelling must be built on the piece of land. But with
the sudden availability after Independence of immense amounts

of federal land for settlement, this concept was gradually abandoned. In the new territories in the West, land was acquired purely for speculation and its distant owner neither lived on it nor worked it. Other pieces of federal land were often occupied by squatters who neither bought it or worked it, and still other land was exploited for its timber or its grazing by persons who neither lived on it nor bothered to buy it. This is how a writer on land use in America sums up the situation. After 1812, he says, "We meet for the first time on a large scale one of the significant realities to which folk myth has blinded us; independence of the three variables: transfer of land from federal title, actual settlement, and economic development." [1]

As a result of this change, land ceased to indicate the status of the owner or occupant or user. Environmentalists are fond of talking about the need of a bond between man and the land, a biological tie or a mystic relationship. But in the traditional landscape, that bond meant something very specific: it meant that a family was legally and economically and even historically identified with the land it owned and lived on and exploited. The bond was the basis of citizenship. Finally, the house itself symbolized the family attachment, and was, in a sense, the matrix of the landscape.

Thus, when that three-fold bond began to lose its power in the course of the 19th Century, the landscape *had* to change. Land was defined in a new way: as a commodity which could be bought and sold and used in a variety of money-making ways, and the house was redefined in much simpler terms: as a place of residence, to be designed and located as such. Home and place of work were no longer necessarily identical and were even sometimes far apart. Land was put to new and unpredictable uses, or left untouched for future speculation. The fabric of the traditional landscape became loose and threatened to fall apart.

It is when we try to follow this development that we discover the importance of a landscape element which we had previously paid little attention to, and that is the road or highway. It had always been there, of course, but it had been so modest, so limited in its influence that we had taken it for granted. For

centuries the country road had been merely a path, a cleared
space created by some local ordinance to enable people to come
to town to pay taxes, go to church, go to market — a political
device, as it were, never given any but the most perfunctory
care. But shortly after the Revolution, the building of roads
became a matter of national concern, and from then on it began
to play a role in the landscape, until (as we all know) it is
now the most powerful force for the destruction or creation of
landscapes that we have.

There is an enormous amount of writing on roads and rail-
ways, and some of it — not all of it by any means — makes
interesting reading. But naturally enough most of it deals with
either the engineering aspect, or with the traffic which the
highway handles, and it is full of superlatives and statistics.
When I first decided to discuss the road, I was sure that it
could be disposed of in two lectures, illustrated with appropriate
slides contrasting old, narrow, rutted roads with the Interstate.
But I soon found out that from the point of view of the course,
the really significant thing about the road was how it affected
the landscape; how it started out as a wavering line between
fields and houses and hills and then took over more and more
land, influenced and changed a wider and wider environment
until the map of the United States seemed nothing but a web of
roads and railroads and highways.

And to further complicate matters, I began to see how the
road altered not only the way people travelled, but how they
perceived the world. The first turnpikes, in the early years
of the 19th Century, gave the youth of America its first taste
of speed: sulky racing got its start on the turnpikes of New
York State, and other turnpikes, by travelling straight across
country and bypassing the small villages, revealed the wilderness aspect of the American landscape. The cult of new models
and accessories and driving techniques got its start when travelers learned to admire the handsomely painted stage coaches
and the shiny harness and the bells on the horses, and when
stage coach drivers competed in style and elegance. The railroad
made an even more profound impression: its business methods
in those days were the first glimpse most Americans had had

of the efficiency of big business, and they were widely imitated. Hard as it is to believe, it was the railroad which taught Americans to be punctual and to watch the clock, and the intricate maneuvering of trains on a single track taught many manufacturers how to organize production and movement.

The automobile, especially in its early days, introduced the notion of exploration. Remote country villages, mountain trails and the trackless regions of the West were rediscovered by adventurous drivers, and there was talk about the revival of the countryside with country inns and country food.

I suspect that each of these experiences of the road increasingly revealed the abstract joys of relatively effortless fast motion, so that in a sense we were psychologically prepared, even a century ago, for surfing and skiing and kite sailing and even skateboarding.

But the road soon began to change the landscape itself. When the railroad came into a town it destroyed the uniformity of the grid system. Railroad Avenue, with its skid row and its hotels, and with its railside factories and warehouses, introduced an axial development and distorted the original spatial order. The streetcar had much the same effect: it extended the range of commuters and gave them a wider choice of places to live, it decentralized many small businesses, and at transfer points it fostered a cluster of stores and services. And the street itself began to assume a new role: the practice of placing utilities under the street pavement — water, gas, sewerage, light, and eventually telephone lines — gave the street a permanence which it had never previously had, so that it became more important than the property on both sides of it. As in almost every other part of the landscape, the road or street or highway became the armature, the framework of the landscape. The piece of land no longer determined its composition.

What I am saying is an old story. We know, because we see evidence of it every day, that the street or highway is like a magnet that attracts houses, factories, places of business and entertainment to its margins. We are all aware that the important streets and arteries no longer exist to serve the local population, but that they create their own community, their own architecture, their own kind of business, their own rhythm and their own mobile population. I have found, somewhat to my embarrassment, that students are, generally speaking, far better informed about the highway and its culture than I am, and if there is any risk in discussing the topic, it is the risk of too much enthusiasm, too great a readiness to describe the drive-in, the truck stop, the advertising, and the psychology of the mobile consumer as forms of pop culture, as topics important and attractive in themselves.

That is one reason why I think the emphasis should be put not so much on the road or highway, as on the broader landscape created or influenced by the highway. For the highway is merely a symbol of how we have learned to organize space and movement; and our zeal to reduce every action, every undertaking to a process of steady, uninterrupted flow of energy and productivity is actually better illustrated in the organization of a factory, a farm, even a university than it is in the incessant activity of the highway. It is in that broader landscape that we can study how the dwelling partakes of the spirit of the highway, and the history of the dwelling over the last one hundred and fifty years demonstrates the slow emergence of new ideas of community and of mobility. The balloon frame was not the outcome of a gradual evolution of folk building techniques; it was invented by harassed carpenters in boomtown Chicago. It rejected tradition and group collaboration in favor of speed and impermanence. The prefabricated or ready cut house, developed in the mid-century, was popularized by the expansion of railroad lines into the treeless High Plains, and made rapid settlement possible. The latest innovation in the dwelling, the trailer, was a response to the need of the motorist for a mobile home. The time has not yet come when we can define the contemporary American home with any finality — in this instance we are indeed in a period of intellectual transition, still thinking of the traditional European dwelling. But the geographers' point is still valid: the house is in many ways a microcosm of the landscape; the landscape explains the house. So let me, in finishing, suggest how the spatial organization of the two landscapes differ — and how in consequence the two types of dwelling differ and could be defined.

The old spatial organization, as I mentioned earlier, laid great store on the visible and permanent divisions of space — whether on the land, or in the house or city; contemporary space is no less well-defined, but the divisions are seen as temporary, and communication between them is essential; the dwelling favors the open plan.

Spatial divisions often meant permanent social distinctions, and autonomous organizations of work: the farm grew and processed and stored and disposed of its own products; the household was an autonomous society responsible for the education, health and welfare of its members. We now delegate various stages in a process to another space — or another institution: the processing plant, the packing plant, the wholesale distributor, and so on — and of course, we delegate domestic responsibilities to the school, the hospital, the various service agencies.

The old spatial organization made much of the need for storage, for provisions for the future, for preserving elements of the past — in barns and attics and warehouses. The modern spatial organization dispenses, whenever possible, with storage space. The supermarket, the factory, the commercial farm depend on trucks either to remove stock or replenish it. The modern dwelling, without attic or cellar, depends on the mini-storage facility or gives every old item to the local museum or to the Goodwill outlet.

And finally, I would say that the old landscape was conservative and even unimaginative in the use of energy; it saw no further than the visible horizon, and was skeptical as to the existence of sources of energy hidden in the ground or untapped within the individual. As for the modern demand for all kinds of energy in unlimited quantities, the daily paper tells us enough about that. But there are other forms of energy which the past knew nothing about — inexhaustible energy which we are seeking to tap by means of spiritual discipline, self-education, and a new experience of nature. The contemporary dwelling, for all its cultural impoverishment, for all its temporary, mobile, rootless qualities, promises to capture and utilize more and more of this invisible, inexhaustible store of strength. So we can perhaps think of it as a transformer: a structure which does more than depend on the energy provided by the power company, which transforms for each of its inhabitants some of that invisible, spiritual energy we are only now beginning to discover.

References

Learning about Landscapes

1. Michel de Montaigne: *Journal de Voyage*, 1770.
2. Michel Foucault: *The Order of Things*, 1973.

Nearer Than Eden

1. C. Reinhold Noyes: *The Institution of Property*, 1936.
2. Karl-Siegfried Bader: *Dorfgenossenschaft*, 1962.
3. F. W. Emery: "England circa 1600," in *A New Historical Geography of England*, 1936.
4. Marc Bloch: *French Rural History*, 1966.
5. Berthold von Regensburg, quoted in G. G. Coulton: *The Medieval Village*, 1931.
6. E. L. Jones: "Creative Disruptions 1620–1820," in *Agricultural History*, October 1974.

Gardens to Decipher and Gardens to Admire

1. Edmund Gosse: "Elizabethan Flower Gardens," in *Harper's Monthly*, June 1905.
2. Geoffrey Grigson: *Gardenage*, 1952.
3. Moriz Heyne: *Das deutsche Wohnungswesen*, 1899.
4. Robert Burton: *The Anatomy of Melancholy*, 1621.
5. Paracelsus: *Selected Writings*, edited by Jolande Jacobi, 1951.
6. Anonymous: *The Perfuming of Tobacco*, 1611.
7. Gosse: "Elizabethan Flower Gardens."
8. Olivier de Serres: *Le Théâtre d'Agriculture et Mesnage des Champs*, 1600.

9. Karl F. W. Jenssen: *Botanik der Gegenwart und Vorzeit,* 1864.
10. Pierre Vallet: *Le Jardin du Roy Tres Chrestien Henry IV,* 1608.
11. Michel Foucault: *The Order of Things,* 1973.
12. Heinrich Wolfflin: *Renaissance und Barock,* 1888.
13. Oswald Spengler: *The Decline of the West,* vol. II, 1928.
14. Gosse: "Elizabethan Flower Gardens."
15. Dieter Hennebo and Alfred Hoffman: *Der Architektonische Garten,* 1965.
16. Gaston Bardet: *Connaissance et Méconaissance de l'Urbanisme,* 1953.

Discovery of the Street

1. Jacques Ellul: *Histoire des Institutions,* 1967.
2. James Vance, Jr.: *This Scene of Man,* 1977.
3. Lynn White, Jr.: *Medieval Technology and Social Change,* 1962
4. Erich Herzog: *Die Ottonische Stadt,* 1964.
5. Oswald Spengler: *The Decline of the West,* vol. II, 1928.

The Sacred Grove

1. Martin P. Nilsson: *Greek Piety,* 1969.
2. Mircea Eliade: *Cosmos and History,* 1954.
3. Cotton Mather: *Magnalia Christi Americana,* 1702.
4. Edwin Scott Gaustad: *Dissent in American Religion,* 1973.
5. Alexander Garden: "Regeneration and the Testimony of the Spirit," quoted in Alan Heimert and Perry Miller, *The Great Awakening,* 1967.
6. Sattivel Quincy: "The Nature and Necessity of Regeneration," quoted in Heimert and Miller.
7. Anonymous: "The Wonderful Wandering Spirit," quoted in Heimert and Miller.
8. W. C. Bryant.
9. Heimert and Miller: *The Great Awakening.*
10. James B. Finley: *Autobiography,* 1853.
11. *The New York Evangelist,* 1835.

The Necessity for Ruins

1. Leopold Eidlitz: *Nature and Function in Art,* 1881.
2. *Landscape,* Winter 1961–62.

The Domestication of the Garage

1. Mel Scott: *American City Planning Since 1890,* 1969.

By Way of Conclusion

1. Thomas Leduc: "History and Appraisal of U.S. Land Policy to 1862," in *Land Use Policy and Problems in the U.S.,* 1963.

Library of Congress Cataloging in Publication Data
Jackson, John Brinckerhoff 1909–
The necessity for ruins, and other topics.
Bibliography: p.
1. Landscape assessment—United States—Addresses,
essays, lectures. 2. United States—Description and
travel—Addresses, essays, lectures. I. Title.
GF91.U6J32   917.3   79-23212
ISBN 0-87023-291-6